CELEBRATING SORROW

CELEBRATING SORROW

MEDIEVAL TRIBUTES TO
THE TALE OF SAGOROMO

INTRODUCTION, TRANSLATIONS, AND ANNOTATIONS BY CHARO B. D'ETCHEVERRY

CORNELL EAST ASIA SERIES
AN IMPRINT OF CORNELL UNIVERSITY PRESS
Ithaca and London

Number 205 in the Cornell East Asia Series

First published 2022 by Cornell University Press

Library of Congress Cataloging-in-Publication Data

Names: D'Etcheverry, Charo Beatrice, 1971– author.
Title: Celebrating sorrow : Medieval tributes to "The tale of Sagoromo" / introduction, translations, and annotations by Charo B. D'Etcheverry.
Description: Ithaca [New York] : Cornell University Press, 2022. | Series: Cornell East Asia series ; number 205 | Includes bibliographical references and index. | Summary: "Celebrating Sorrow presents annotated translations from seven medieval Japanese works highlighting the eleventh-century Tale of Sagoromo, revealing how later authors, teachers, and commentarists used the tale to depict and navigate the chaotic era between the fall of the Heian court and the rise of the Tokugawa shogunate."— Provided by publisher.
Identifiers: LCCN 2021062609 (print) | LCCN 2021062610 (ebook) | ISBN 9781501764776 (hardcover) | ISBN 9781501764790 (pdf) | ISBN 9781501764783 (epub)
Subjects: LCSH: Rokujō Saiin no Senji, –1092. Sagoromo monogatari—Influence. | Japanese literature—1185–1600—History and criticism.
Classification: LCC PL726.3 .D48 2022 (print) | LCC PL726.3 (ebook) | DDC 895.63/14—dc23/eng/20220406
LC record available at https://lccn.loc.gov/2021062609
LC ebook record available at https://lccn.loc.gov/2021062610

Contents

ACKNOWLEDGMENTS

This book would not exist without the support of several institutions and many generous individuals, including those I am privileged to thank here. Naturally, I take credit for any lingering infelicities and mistakes.

At the University of Wisconsin, I received related funding for one summer, courtesy of the Graduate School Research Competition, and a semester's project assistant, part of a Vilas Life Cycle Professorship. That award also funded a short trip to Japan, during which I collected some materials used in this book, while the staff at Memorial Library chased down the rest. In the Department of Asian Languages and Cultures (formerly East Asian Languages and Literatures), Rania Huntington gave helpful feedback on the introduction, while Steve Ridgely made a suggestion that improved the entire book. William Nienhauser Jr. located a translation of a Chinese verse noted in chapter 4, and former project assistant Kenia Avendaño-Garro cheered me on throughout. Outside of my department, Sarah Thal, Lee Wandel, Yoriko Dixon, and Susan Zaeske offered an invaluable mixture of encouragement and straight talk.

I also benefited from help further afield. Edwin and Fumiko Cranston have long supported my work on *Sagoromo*. Reggie Jackson invited me to present some material related to this book at a workshop held at the University of Chicago, where I received helpful feedback, particularly from Terry Kawashima and Wayne Farris. While teaching on the Associated Kyoto Program, I met Sachiko Kawasaki of Ritsumeikan University, who clarified a point tied to chapter 5 and gave me a second copy of her book on *The Tale of Sagoromo*'s reception, so that I could consult it at home and the office. Mai Shaikhanuar-Cota was a fountain of good advice at Cornell East Asia Series, as were the CEAS Board and its outside reviewers; when Cornell University Press absorbed CEAS, Alexis Siemon tactfully guided this project to completion. She also ensured that readers could see the crucial part of the cover image, used with the permission of the Art Institute of Chicago ® under a Creative Commons license. I hope that all of these people and the many others not named here, who asked helpful questions at conferences or in conversation, know how much I appreciated their advice.

My warmest thanks go to my husband and son, Jody and Cooper Shaw. Like most books, this one represents years of effort, much of it performed at times when "most mothers" (per Cooper) would not be at work. His complaint reminds me that this project coincided with a difficult period for our family, even before COVID struck. If that timing partially explains my approach to my materials, as windows onto other people navigating upheavals in their own lives, it also means that I was not as available to my loved ones as they might have hoped. I am sorry for shutting my office door so often, guys. Let's get Wani and go for a walk.

ABBREVIATIONS

KCS	*Kokubungaku chūshaku sōsho*
KKT	*Kōchū kokka taikei*
KYS	*Kōchū yōkyoku sōsho*
NKBT	*Nihon koten bungaku taikei*
NMZ	*Nihon meicho zenshū*
OMS	*Ōchō monogatari shūkasen*
SMKR	*Sagoromo monogatari kyōjushi ronkyū*
SNKS	*Shinchō Nihon koten shūsei*
SNKZ	*Shinpen Nihon koten bungaku zenshū*
SZ	*Sōka zenshishū*

NOTE ON CONVENTIONS

My quotations from *The Tale of Sagoromo* reflect the modernized text in *SNKS*, the only major series to use a circulating version of the tale and the closest to the copies that inform the tributes. This edition is based on a copy of a manuscript dated to the late Muromachi period (1336–1573). I also lead with *SNKS* in most notes, excepting in chapter 3, where the work presented favors the older manuscript presented in *NKBT*, otherwise listed in second place. For ease of reference, I also key to the hybrid version in *SNKZ*, the most widely held edition of the tale and with the newest annotations in these three series. This *Sagoromo* also contains pictures and a running translation in modern Japanese, making it the most accessible version for the modern audience.

While I generally cite published English versions of Japanese works when available, all *Sagoromo*-themed translations are my own. In the spirit of accessibility, I refer to Japanese texts by the common English titles or (for less familiar texts) literal translations used here after first reference. I also borrow Steven Hanna's names for the tale's major characters, as seen in his forthcoming translation from Cornell University Press. Since sobriquets change over the course of the original work, I give the traditional Japanese names in parentheses (when different from Hanna's names) when I first mention the character. References to court offices otherwise follow *The Princeton Companion to Japanese Literature*, from which I borrow the English titles for most literary works. Unlike *Companion*, I hyphenate names that recall earlier rulers (e.g., Go-Saga, not Gosaga), with the exception of Koichijō-in, who never took the throne and whose name refers most directly to his residence. When presenting Japanese script, I use modern kanji. I also transliterate according to modern usage (e.g., *ōi*, not *ohoi*).

I am thrilled that this volume will be available as an e-book. To help those readers locate cross-referenced poems quickly, I supply the transliterated first line (or, when needed, the first two lines) of such verses parenthetically, after noting where the full text and translations appear in the book (regardless of format). People using the e-version should be able to copy and paste these lines into the search engine to find the full poem with minimal difficulty, while readers of the print version can flip to the appendices and find it there. While I cite a number of poems from other sources in the notes, and a few more appear in the translations themselves, I have restricted the related appendix to poems taken from *Sagoromo* or seemingly inspired by it.

Introduction

What happens when social orders collapse? This book of translations offers glimpses from Japan's medieval era, the four centuries between the fall of the Heian court (794–1185), located in what we call Kyoto, and the rise of the Tokugawa shogunate (1603–1868) in Edo, now Tokyo. These years brought intermittent civil war, inspiring a national literature built on shared stories but also on the fracture of works like *The Tale of Sagoromo* (*Sagoromo monogatari*, ca. 1070), traditionally ranked with *The Tale of Genji* (*Genji monogatari*, ca. 1010) for its elegant prose and *waka* verse.[1] The "tributes" to *Sagoromo* presented here—a short narrative, from a cycle of similar works that comprise the lone prose adaptation; forty-one of its poems as cited by two compilers, with their headnotes (*kotobagaki*) contextualizing each verse; three libretti, from the only known *Sagoromo*-based songs and surviving play; and the beginning of the leading commentary—thus trace more than the medieval reception of one work. They also suggest how generations

---

1. See Ruch, "Medieval Jongleurs and the Making of a National Literature." Put simply, *waka* are Japanese-language poems in roughly thirty-one syllables. For a more detailed introduction to this genre, and to the related art of *renga* mentioned below, see Carter, *How to Read a Japanese Poem*. My reference to the "fracture" or fragmentary use of courtly works, elaborated on below, is inspired by David Pollack's discussion of the role of China in early definitions of Japanese identity; see *The Fracture of Meaning* for details. However, in the present case, particular works (more precisely, their words and phrases) matter as much as the dialectic he discusses.

of literate people coped with upheaval: by lamenting or justifying it in familiar terms, unraveling a tale paradoxically known for its coherence.

Even for a premodern work, *Sagoromo* spans a diverse corpus of texts. Before the spread of woodblock printing in the seventeenth century, Japanese literature circulated in manuscript, sparking revisions on top of the inevitable scribal errors until preferred versions took root. *Sagoromo* spurred great enthusiasm but no such default, leading to numerous "copies" that vary widely in some aspects: for instance, in the divisions among the tale's four untitled books (book 1 sometimes ends with a cliff-hanger), the characterization of minor figures, and the roughly 213 *waka*, tied to emotionally charged scenes as typical in courtly works.[2] The tale's style also shifts across copies, with the oldest extant, thirteenth-century versions (*kohon*) featuring long sentences and allusions abridged in popular circulating texts (*rufubon*). This trend toward simplicity reflects *Sagoromo*'s growing audience over the medieval period, also seen in the pronunciation guides (*furigana*) added to some copies. Meanwhile, the plot stayed the same, spanning twelve years in the life of a fictional nobleman, or one round of the courtly zodiac.

True to that scheme, in which five rounds mark rebirth, *Sagoromo* ends with signs of a new cycle but no fresh start. The hero whom we first meet in spring, later identified as the eighteen-year-old Genji or "new commoner" Middle Captain (*Gen chūjō*), has married the doppelganger of the woman he wants after evading one unwanted bride and outliving another (she becomes a nun and then dies, like his first narrated lover).[3] He is also the emperor, having been enthroned by the sun-goddess Amaterasu, mythic ancestor of the imperial house, while his father—demoted from princely status before the hero's birth—becomes a retired emperor, on the principle that a ruler's parents should hold imperial rank. Accordingly, while deities praise the hero's talents throughout the tale, Amaterasu only puts him on the throne in book 4, when his son by a princess, secretly raised as her brother, is poised to join the succession and compromise the imperial line. We leave the hero brooding in autumn, a season poetically opposed to spring; where spring marks new love, fall suggests surfeit.[4] His problem is attachment, always excessive in the tale's Buddhist outlook.

---

2. The exact number of poems in *Sagoromo* varies. For instance, while Sugiura Noriko notes that a widely used database of *waka* lists 210 poems for *Sagoromo*, she counts 216 in her preferred edition, based on older texts; see Sugiura, "*Sagoromo monogatari* ni okeru waka no igi." I give the average of these two figures here.

3. As detailed below, *Sagoromo* starts in media res. While the tale later hints at earlier affairs, including one with the Crown Prince's consort (known as the Sen'yōden for her palace apartments), the first narrated liaison involves a poor woman discussed below.

4. The word for fall, *aki*, puns on the classical verb *aku*, to become disgusted with.

As his choice of wife betrays, the hero still desires his first object: his foster sister, now a priestess at the Kamo Shrine, which protects the court. Since affairs with priestesses are taboo in any case, the hero's continued passion portends disaster, also signaled by his wife's final titles: originally known as the daughter of the former Minister of Ceremonial (*Shikibukyō no Miya*), another unsuccessful prince, she becomes the new emperor's Fujitsubo Consort and Fujitsubo Empress (*Fujitsubo no Nyōgo, Fujitsubo no Chūgū*), names synonymous with failed substitutes and betrayal in *Genji*.[5] This thread loosely recalls the hero's father, who may have been demoted for seducing another priestess, the hero's mother; the narrator speculates that the older man committed a "crime" (*tsumi*) in the past, since both of his full brothers became emperors. Either way, the hero resembles his father in his lack of restraint, weeping in the end because he failed to seduce a nun, the mother of the "prince" who triggered his promotion.[6] Here as elsewhere, the tale comes nearly full circle, eschewing renewal for what translator Steven Hanna calls "traps": the bonds of desire that structure the plot and, in Buddhist terms, preclude enlightenment.[7]

This tightly woven narrative, preserved even in simplified circulating texts, sets *Sagoromo* apart among Heian tales. Many of its poems also resonate with each other across subplots, further unifying the work. One of Japan's first modern literary critics thus deemed it the highpoint of courtly fiction, despite calling *Genji* the genre's signal accomplishment for its greater realism and length.[8] Nonetheless, medieval writers unraveled *Sagoromo*, engaging with different strands of it or putting the same threads to different uses as their worlds "turned upside down" during war and political realignments.[9] For example, late twelfth- and thirteenth-century poets with connections to the palace included the tale's saddest poems in two influential sets

---

5. In *Genji*, the hero's imperial father marries the doppelganger of the hero's dead mother, assigning the new woman to the Fujitsubo (Wisteria Pavilion) at the palace. The infatuated hero then pursues her nieces, one of whom closely resembles her, just as his (nominal) son Kaoru pursues the sisters of a dead woman whom he loved. None of these relationships ends well.

6. Alternatively, this may suggest an impending golden age led by the hero and his sister, since court myth includes married sibling-rulers: notably, the legendary shaman Himiko (also Pimiko), who conveyed the gods' will to her brother, who then ruled the kingdom on her behalf. On the symbolic relationship between emperors and Kamo priestesses in particular, see Faure, *The Power of Denial*, 294–96.

7. See Hanna, "Hemmed In."

8. See Fujioka, *Kokubungaku zenshi*, 528. He ties *Genji*'s more sustained portrait of its hero and his milieu to its allegedly novelistic ethos, his benchmark for judging literary history. *Genji* spans about seventy years and is three or four times *Sagoromo*'s length.

9. The phrase in quotation marks, from the fifteenth-century term *gekokujō*, appears in the title of Pierre Souyri's 1998 study of the period, *The World Turned Upside Down*, as translated by Käthe Roth. Some scholars have rejected this view as anachronistic, instead emphasizing continuities like the shared recourse to courtly works considered here; for instance, see Butler, "The Riches of

of *waka* meant to train their students and celebrate courtly tales (as noted, these genres overlap). By the fourteenth century, an obscure monk in the military capital of Kamakura had combined phrases from many of these poems with bits of the tale's exposition to create two banquet songs (*sōka* or *enkyoku*), sung for shoguns by lesser warriors and nobles and evoking trips to this center of patronage and employment. As my summaries suggest, both the songs and the selections of verse inspire pity, but their purposes differ, as do their presentations of the shared content.

Later writers pulled other threads from *Sagoromo*, even as the earlier tributes continued to circulate. Notable here, in the late fifteenth century, a courtier drafted a ghost play (*mugen nō*) for one Kyoto-based shogun, later staged for another, highlighting the tonsured princess and her formerly splendid garments. Meanwhile, anonymous writers turned the arc about the hero's lover into a cycle of short narratives (*Muromachi jidai monogatari*) with competing happy endings and bathetic details: for instance, a poem comparing orphans to hen-pecked chickens. Finally, as the sixteenth century ended, a lowborn master of *renga*—linked verse, based on *waka*—wrote a commentary on the tale for an ambitious warlord, glossing the poems and confusing points in the exposition like earlier guides, but only after evoking a hidden theme: that the gods assist all worthy men, not just aristocrats. Like their precursors, these writers matched *Sagoromo* to new fears and desires, suggesting their mixed feelings about change itself.[10]

Tellingly, while some of these tributes circulated more widely than others, medieval readers preserved all of them, indicating that each work met needs not filled by the rest. In fact, as seen in my notes to the translations, some authors drew on the others' compositions, underscoring their distinct visions and goals in the process. In this sense, the present book traces *Sagoromo*'s role in the national literature noted earlier, as a shared source of phrases and themes rather than a shared story.[11] This usage recalls that of other Heian

---

Medieval Japanese Society." However, I find that *Sagoromo*-themed works at least echo the perception of dramatic change, by repeatedly tying parts of the tale to new, often challenging circumstances.

10. See Ebersole, "The Poetics and Politics of Ritualized Weeping," for a thoughtful discussion of the problems with inferring emotion of any kind from medieval Japanese texts and other early and/or culturally distant sources. While I take his point, I do not have space in the current setting to delve into the historical detail he recommends as a counterweight.

11. While *Sagoromo*'s readership grew over the medieval era, as noted, parts of the short narratives (for instance, their abbreviated account of how the hero got his name, discussed below) suggest that their audience had only a rudimentary understanding of the tale's plot. The many copies of those works, as well as the triumphal nature of some early modern illustrations of the tale itself, point to *Sagoromo*'s role in what Ruch later called the common culture, rather than as a shared story as such. See Ruch, "The Other Side of Culture," especially the conclusion.

narratives, notably *Genji* and *Tales of Ise* (*Ise monogatari*, early tenth century), another influence on *Sagoromo* also favored by poets. In all three cases, medieval writers shrunk the work to their favorite elements, deployed according to their own needs and tastes.[12]

That said, fewer authors relied on *Sagoromo* than on the other tales, despite its comparable prestige. In fact, while medieval vernacular literature contains many references and allusions to the featured work, the present volume spans most of the extant long-form treatments of it. As noted, I include excerpts from the leading commentary and present the overlapping poems from the two sets of verse mentioned above, which imply clearer endorsements than the lists of the tale's *waka* also made in this era (since the number of poems varies across texts of *Sagoromo*, the line between deliberate omission and simple ignorance is murky in the latter works).[13] I also translate the only dedicated engagements with the tale extant in other genres and discuss the most important work not presented here: a fictional review already available in English, considered below. To my knowledge, the only other noteworthy tributes are a postscript to some copies of the tale, which I analyze elsewhere,[14] and a genealogy of the characters (*keizu*), mentioned in the featured commentary. While visual art is beyond my scope, few medieval pictures of the tale seem to have endured either.[15]

Given *Sagoromo*'s popularity in the medieval period, the scarcity of tributes probably partly reflects the confusion caused by its diverse corpus. As seen in my excerpt from the commentary, the *renga* master felt compelled to collate his own version of the tale before writing about it, because the copies he borrowed contained so many confusing passages and seeming mistakes. These challenges may also have been the reason that the men whom

---

12. For a broad discussion of *Genji*'s reception, and translations of many examples, see Harper and Shirane, *Reading "The Tale of Genji."* For a close look at *Ise*'s competing commentaries, see Newhard, *Knowing the Amorous Man.*

13. On two earlier collections of the tale's poems, see Sudō, *Sagoromo monogatari juyō no kenkyū*, 58–119. This book also contains transcriptions of a number of relevant works, most of them from the early modern era. On earlier commentaries, as preserved in an annotated copy of the tale in the hand of Sanjōnishi Kin'eda (1487–1563), see Gakushūin Daigaku Heian Bungaku Kenkyūkai, *Sanjōnishi kebon Sagoromo monogatari chūshaku*. As noted below, the author of the commentary featured here studied with Kin'eda's family. Unfortunately, I was not able to consult this volume directly while preparing this introduction, but it is clear from the featured author's comments and later references to his own work that it did not circulate broadly.

14. See D'Etcheverry, "Performing Emotion."

15. The only directly relevant artwork from this era is a damaged early medieval picture scroll held by the Tokyo National Museum that includes passages from the tale. By contrast, there are numerous early modern illustrations, including those printed with the tale, as noted below, in 1654. For a discussion of the early modern materials, including a survey of the scenes covered in that printing, see Takahashi, "*Sagoromo monogatari* genzon ega shiryō bamen ichiran."

he named as authorities did not lecture on the tale, although one of their families preserved earlier exegeses in notes to one copy of it.[16] Serendipity and later tastes also shape the present book. Most of my base texts, identified at the head of each translation with the details of my interventions, derive from early modern copies, while I chose the featured version of the short narrative because I like it. Less intentionally, my work tends to obscure the fact that medieval writers used many different texts of *Sagoromo* because I reference the same three versions of the tale in my notes. See the "note on conventions" for more details on my choices there, balanced between accuracy (here meaning the modern editions closest to the texts cited by medieval authors) and accessibility.

Despite these limitations, the present volume approaches a comprehensive set of sustained references to *Sagoromo* from the thirteenth through sixteenth centuries, illuminating the tale's reception, Japanese history, and human nature alike. While the presumably low rates of literacy in the medieval era mean that these works addressed only a fraction of Japan's population at that time,[17] they also depict variations within this privileged demographic, whose members hailed (as noted earlier) from competing political centers and social groups. Furthermore, despite the diversity of the tale's corpus, the medieval writers' shared recourse to a compact and notably cohesive source makes their shifts in emphasis clearly visible, unlike responses to more expansive works.[18] As a set, these tributes to *Sagoromo* thus yield surprisingly rich insights into how people negotiate change, especially shifts in access to power and wealth. I outline those findings at the end of this introduction, when identifying the works translated here and their known authors and audiences. First, I offer a fuller overview of *Sagoromo*, centered on those elements most popular with medieval writers at large.

---

16. See Sudō, *Sagoromo monogatari juyō no kenkyū*, chap. 1, for a discussion of these lists.

17. Information on literacy rates in the medieval period is notoriously hard to come by. Most discussions of this topic seem to center on whether or not farmers were able to sign their names, a level of skill with words well below that needed to make sense of the complex grammar, vocabulary, and allusions found in courtly works like *Sagoromo*. Given the pronunciation guides noted above, which emerged in later, circulating texts of the tale and also appear in some copies of the short narratives, it is probably safe to say that few people other than aristocrats, leading warriors (often related to nobles), and wealthy commoners knew the tale or its tributes directly.

18. See Harper and Shirane, *Reading "The Tale of Genji."* As that anthology attests, *Genji* was read in canonical texts and through commentaries since at least the early medieval period, in contrast to the freedom of choosing a text from *Sagoromo*'s diverse corpus. While *Sagoromo* seems to have inspired exegeses in the early medieval period, as noted below, these do not have appeared to have circulated very widely. Our *renga* master, for example, does not appear to have had access to them, despite studying with the heir of one of the families that produced them.

Sagoromo: Relevant Background

As I have detailed elsewhere, *Sagoromo* was written by an aristocrat called Senji (d. 1092), the wetnurse and lifelong attendant of Princess Baishi (1039–96), Kamo priestess (*saiin*) for roughly twelve years.[19] Since *Sagoromo* often evokes or cites *Genji*—and because Baishi's guardian Fujiwara no Yorimichi (992–1071) was the son of Michinaga (966–1028), who hired *Genji* author Murasaki Shikibu (ca. 978–?)—many early readers credited *Sagoromo* to Murasaki's daughter, another imperial nurse; indeed, we see this attribution in the featured commentary. Critics now stress Senji's distinct talents and interests, often linked to Baishi's time at the shrine. While that period shaped *Sagoromo*, as the tale's chronology and the Kamo God's role in the plot indicate, medieval writers stressed Senji's poetic skills, an even larger part of her life.

Like the rest of her adoptive family, Baishi sponsored numerous poem contests (*utaawase*), which her staff organized and in which they took part. Most relevant here is a 1055 "tale-poem contest" (*monogatari utaawase*) that matched verse from short tales written for the event. Senji's lost entry, *The Provisional Major Counselor Who Dallied in Jewelweed* (*Tamamo ni asobu gondainagon*), apparently began by stating its theme rather than with the usual introduction to the hero's family, an innovation reprised in *Sagoromo*; the first tale is considered a study for the second, based on the reviews of both works in *The Nameless Book* (*Mumyōzōshi*, ca. 1201). Like the featured tributes, this fictional conversation among nuns was written by someone who also wrote verse, in this case, an active practitioner of *waka* and *renga* known as Shunzei's Daughter (ca. 1171–ca. 1252). Accordingly, her characters quote poems throughout the conversation and warmly praise *Genji*, which Fujiwara Shunzei (1114–1204)—actually the author's grandfather and a leading *waka* theorist—called required reading for poets while judging a contest.[20] When one of the nuns brings up *Sagoromo*, opining that it "ranks [next] after *Genji*,"[21] we can thus assume that the compliment includes Senji's verse.

The Nameless Book also, however, highlights other parts of *Sagoromo*, which further bolstered its categorization with *Genji*, *Ise*, and imperial anthologies of verse (*chokusenshū*) as a resource for poets. Judging from the nuns' comments, Shunzei's Daughter set great store by Senji's use of allusion, a poetic

---

19. See D'Etcheverry, *Love after "The Tale of Genji,"* chap. 1.
20. See the discussion of *Poetry Contest in Six Hundred Rounds* (*Roppyakuban utaawase*, 1193) in Atkins, *Teika*, chap. 2.
21. Trans. Marra, "Part 2," 292. For the Japanese, see Kuwabara, *Mumyōzōshi*, 58.

technique again prized by Shunzei.[22] The review's first extract from *Sagoromo* is particularly telling in this sense. Regardless of the copy, the tale usually begins, "The springtime of youth (*shōnen no haru*) is fleeting," evoking a couplet by China's Bai Juyi (772–846): "Back to the candle, together we cherish / the moon late in the night; / treading on petals, we share lamentation / for *the springtime of our youth*" (emphasis added).[23] Shunzei's Daughter began her review of the tale by quoting just the first phrase, italicized in the preceding couplet, although she presumably knew the rest of the line and may have had access to a version of the tale that began more like *Genji*.[24] Here and elsewhere, the nuns stress Senji's poetic skills, extolling the excerpt as an example of her "wonderfully noble style"—the key term here is *en*, another of Shunzei's favorite topics—while dismissing the tale's plot as uncompelling and filled with miraculous events that one "may prefer not to see there."[25]

The Nameless Book also previews the medieval preference for the theme of romantic longing (*koi*), a staple of imperial anthologies and court tales alike. The rest of *Sagoromo*'s first sentence sets the scene in the Third Month (late spring by the court's lunar calendar), illustrating the initial claim about the passage of time. The next line shows the still unnamed hero staring at a garden as he yearns for his foster sister, a maternal cousin later introduced as the Genji Princess (*Genji no Miya*); in this case, the "new commoner" label marks her adoption by his parents, who have promised her to his paternal cousin, the Crown Prince. Since Bai's couplet focuses on shared regrets (hence the translators' addition of the plural pronoun), the allusion sets off the hero's isolation. His related longing for his sister, only one of the attachments noted above, spurred his traditional sobriquet, assigned by readers from one of his poems.

While Shunzei's Daughter did not cite that verse, it is worth quoting here, since it sets up the strands of the tale most visible in medieval tributes. The poem appears early in book 1, not long after the hero is forced to play his

22. In addition to Atkins and Carter, noted earlier on Shunzei's views, see Shirane, "Lyricism and Intertextuality."

23. Excerpted in *Collection of Japanese and Chinese Poems to Sing* (*Wakan rōeishū*, ca. 1013). Trans. Rimer and Chaves, *Japanese and Chinese Poems*, 34.

24. Shimizu Hamaomi (1776–1824) noted the existence of this old copy, apparently by the court lady Nijō-in no Sanuki (ca. 1141–1217), which began with the hero's parents and then circled back to the current thematic opener; see Toki, "*Sagoromo monogatari bōtō*," 11. As Sanuki was a contemporary of Shunzei and his son Teika (discussed below), both of whom put her poems in their collections, Shunzei's Daughter may have known of this version of the tale.

25. Trans. Marra, "Part 2," 292; Kuwabara, *Mumyōzōshi*, 59. On *en*, often translated as "charm," see the glossary in Carter, *How to Read a Japanese Poem*. I discuss the objectionable events briefly below and at greater length in "Performing Emotion."

flute for his uncle, the Saga Emperor (named by readers for the site of his retirement villa, where the tale ends). The hero's skillful performance attracts the god of music Amewakamiko,[26] inspiring the woodblock print by artist Yashima Gakutei (ca. 1786–1868) shown on the cover of this book: *Sagoromo* (ca. 1820), from the series *Ten Courtly Tales for the Honcho Circle* (*Honchōren monogatari jūban*).[27] This episode informs the extant play, which ends with Amewakamiko's dance. While Gakutei's print and some texts of the tale depict a goddess, the important narrative detail is the deity's attempt to give the hero a heavenly feathered robe (*ama no hagoromo*), in which to rise to the sky, escaping his sorrows at the palace. The Saga Emperor prevents this, then recites a *waka* punning on "straw raincoat" (*minoshiro*) to offer a "personal substitute" for the garment: his favorite daughter, the Second Princess (*Ni no Miya*), introduced above as the mother of the hero's first son.[28] This proposal spurs the crucial poem, which even gave the tale its title, often simply "*Sagoromo*" in medieval works like *The Nameless Book*.

As a mere courtier, the hero cannot refuse the Saga Emperor's offer, but he never accepts it, despite his later liaison with the Princess. Instead, determined not to rule out a marriage to his sister, he makes a polite but ambiguous reply, continuing the textile metaphor to hint at his true feelings,[29] then recites a second, defiant verse when he gets home:

色々に重ねては着じ人知れず思ひそめてしよは の狭衣

One color atop	*iro iro ni*
another I will not wear;	*kasanete wa kiji*
though I hide the truth,	*hito shirezu*
it already bears love's hue,	*omoisometeshi*
this narrow robe worn at night.[30]	*yowa no sagoromo*

Here he swears not to touch the Second Princess, symbolized by the colorfully layered robes typical of feminine courtly dress; as he says, his robe is already dyed with love for his sister. Since lovers ideally slept together, beneath their shed clothing, the poem also constitutes a vow to sleep alone

---

26. For more on this deity, see Reider, "A Demon in the Sky."

27. At around the same time, Gakutei also produced another print on this theme, *The Sagoromo Major Captain* (*Sagoromo no taishō*), from the series *Three Gentlemen of Japanese Literature* (*Washo sankōshi*). While the deity there looks different, the hero is still playing his flute. Both prints also contain new poems, confirming the tale's continued association with verse.

28. For this verse, see my notes to "Sagoromo's Sleeves" in chapter 3 (*mi no shiro mo*).

29. For this verse, see my notes to the short narrative in chapter 1 (*murasaki no*).

30. *SNKS* 1:41.

in his *sagoromo*, the poetic term for robes in general, otherwise called *koromo* or *kinu*. Medieval readers seized on this word and the related theme of longing, calling the hero "the Sagoromo Middle Captain," "the Sagoromo Emperor," and "the Sagoromo Major Captain" (*Taishō*), with the last name referencing his only intervening post before his enthronement. My translation of the poem, meanwhile, reflects a common transcription of the shared term, which presents the first syllable, the poetic prefix *sa*, with the Chinese character for "narrow," adding a sense of entrapment that recalls the hero's command performance.[31] While copyists and later writers seem to have used these transcriptions interchangeably, medieval writers stressed the hero's attempts to choose his path, suggesting that this meaning resonated in plain transcriptions of the sobriquet, too.

One more broad point is useful before turning to medieval writers' favorite parts of the plot. For reasons not made clear to the reader, Sagoromo (as I will call him) does not tell his parents how he feels about his sister, although modern critics argue that he could have married her if he had. Lord Horikawa (*Horikawa no Otodo*) and his wife dote on their only natural child and Horikawa's only son; like many historical Heian noblemen, the Great Minister (*Ōki Otodo*), as Horikawa is also called, also has other wives, with other daughters. Perhaps Sagoromo realizes that his father's career depends on taking imperial sons-in-law, in order to produce malleable reigning grandsons. That strategy ensured Michinaga's success, including Yorimichi's half century as the court's leading minister, and the tale evokes it repeatedly, giving Horikawa one such grandchild by Sagoromo's half sister and describing a third wife's attempt to adopt Horikawa's suspected love child and marry her to a prince.[32] Meanwhile, Sagoromo seeks relief in a series of secret relationships. The most important here are those with the lover noted earlier, a poor orphan called Asukai, and the Second Princess. They are also the major subjects of the tale's first two books.

---

31. One pair of annotators rejects this literal reading of the title, claiming that the related character is used only for its sound; see Matsumura and Ishikawa, "Kaisetsu," 3. On the poetic reference to robes, and to sleeping garments more specifically, see Toyoshima, "Koromo no keifu."

32. For a brief discussion of this subplot, involving Horikawa's wife Lady Tōin (*Tōin no Ue*) and the daughter's governess, see D'Etcheverry, "Out of the Mouths of Nurses," 163–69. This material also appears in slightly different form in D'Etcheverry, *Love after "The Tale of Genji,"* chap. 2. I refer to Lady Tōin in both venues as Lady Dōin, following the pronunciation supplied in *NKBT*, my base text in those studies.

Emphases in the Tributes

Like Sagoromo, Asukai gets her name from a poem, in this case, part of an exchange between the lovers that invokes a spring popular with Heian travelers. The sobriquet foreshadows her own numerous trips. After Sagoromo accidentally foils her kidnapping by a priest, who tricks her into his carriage while she is staying at his temple, Asukai lets the hero escort her home; he then visits her nightly, which would mean marriage by Heian standards if he identified himself. Instead, he hesitates, too worried about what his sister might think even to bring Asukai home as a servant. When her nurse arranges for her to marry his unwitting retainer Michinari, the heroine finds herself forced into another carriage, bound for Michinari's new post in the provinces and already expecting Sagoromo's child. She escapes with the help of her long-lost brother, a priest whose boat is moored beside theirs when she tries to drown herself (the cliff-hanger version of book 1 ends here). Unfortunately, while he tries to find Sagoromo, who is off seeking her, she dies, after giving birth to a daughter and taking the tonsure.

The nuns in *The Nameless Book* love this story, recalling the copyists who preserved or created the cliff-hanger ending and the competing portraits of Asukai's nurse seen throughout the tale's corpus, a sign of the subplot's general popularity.[33] Similarly, despite their disparaging comment about *Sagoromo*'s narrative, the fictional nuns repeatedly praise Asukai and her experiences as "moving" (*aware naru*), quoting poems from the beginning and end of her final trip,[34] although they only cite five *waka* from the tale in total. She is also the only character from the tale whom they quote twice, although Sagoromo writes the vast majority of its verse. Both of the featured poems also appear in the collections presented here, attesting to her broader embrace by poets. Indeed, Asukai appears to outstrip all of the tale's other heroines in those collections, and again by large margins, although since one of my sources is damaged (see below), such judgments must be provisional. In any case, her upstaging of the hero in *The Nameless Book* reveals that medieval poets did not feel compelled to be representative in their choices, and Shunzei's Daughter made Asukai the centerpiece of her review.

---

33. See D'Etcheverry, "Out of the Mouths of Nurses." This material also appears in slightly different form in D'Etcheverry, *Love after "The Tale of Genji*," chap. 2.

34. See Marra, "Part 2," 293–94; Kuwabara, *Mumyōzōshi*, 60–61. Both sources refer to Asukai as Michishiba ("the roadside grasses"), a competing sobriquet also drawn from the subplot. For the featured verses by Asukai, see poems 9 and 13 in chapter 2 (*ama no to o* and *hayaki se no*).

Unsurprisingly, given its acclaim with poets, this arc also inspired two of the tributes featured here. Phrases from its poems and exposition dominate one of the banquet songs, while the short narratives focus on this part of the tale to the exclusion of the rest of it. Indeed, the nuns' remarks anticipate the cycle's major revision to Asukai's story. Their comments on this heroine (and the positive part of the review generally) end with the wish that she had lived longer, to see how much Sagoromo loved her and perhaps to redeem what they call a "disappointing" (kuchioshiki) relationship.[35] As noted, the cycle grants this wish, literally resurrecting Asukai and making her the hero's main wife, replacing a woman chosen for him (in the cycle) by his parents.

Senji instead added a grim denouement, also evoked by medieval writers. While seeking Asukai, Sagoromo chants a sutra so fervently that the bodhisattva Fugen or "Universal Worthy" (in Sanskrit, Samantabhadra) appears, fulfilling a vow to appear to believers but not reuniting the lovers. Instead, the hero finds Asukai's brother, then her daughter and, much later, Asukai's ghost, who appears in a dream in book 4 to reveal that his prayers for her soul did not work. He then turns her diary into a copy of the Nirvana Sutra (J. Nehangyō), dedicating it to her enlightenment since that scripture pledges to help those whom the Lotus Sutra (J. Hokkekyō), normally favored by Heian aristocrats, cannot. This passage led some medieval writers to pair the tale and the Nirvana Sutra, as seen in my excerpt from the commentary, which also invokes Fugen and the Kamo God as deities, not just as characters in the tale. The short narratives, meanwhile—some of which, like my example, praise the Lotus Sutra—describe the lovers as avatars of Buddhist figures, influenced by the belief that those deities take local forms in Japan.[36] Shunzei's Daughter was less impressed with supernatural events. After discussing Asukai, the nuns return to the tale's distasteful miracles, decrying them as "unrealistic" (makotoshikaranu),[37] although they say nothing about the ghost.

Several of the featured tributes also underscore a practical consequence of Asukai's death: her child's adoption by another woman, known in the tale as the Ippon Princess (Ippon no Miya). This event ultimately forces Sagoromo's first marriage, when he is spotted at the Princess's house looking for his daughter and rumors flare that he has seduced her guardian, also a retired Kamo priestess. Since even princesses without shrine connections ideally

---

35. See Marra, "Part 2," 294; Kuwabara, Mumyōzōshi, 61. Marra translates kuchioshiki as "pitiful."
36. On the role of this concept in medieval literature and literary commentaries, see Klein, Allegories of Desire. For a recent broader discussion that also considers such works, see Teeuwen, "The Kami in Esoteric Buddhist Thought and Practice."
37. See Marra, "Part 2," 295; Kuwabara, Mumyōzōshi, 62–63.

stayed single—an expectation that underlines the magnitude of the Saga Emperor's offer of his daughter, even if it was regularly ignored in practice—the rumors threaten to create a scandal, which the marriage (unwelcome to both parties) mitigates. In the tale's closely woven plot, this development again recalls the hero's parents, hinting that Sagoromo might be able to marry his sister once she retires from the shrine, whether she loves him or not.

Instead of discussing this point, *The Nameless Book*—which follows its praise for the tale's opening line with the Ippon Princess, taking the plot out of order as detailed below—simply calls her "impressive" (*imiji*), with a further comment that seems to praise her stoic acceptance of the marriage and perhaps her later tonsure, once she learns that Sagoromo only wants her foster child.[38] Meanwhile, the short narratives highlight the child's suffering, with some of them also making this character a son. My example shows the boy comparing himself unfavorably to the featherless chickens that he sees in the Princess's garden, either a sign of their pecking order or a nod to Heian-era cockfights. Either way, the verse casts a shadow on the adoption, a common tool in Heian and medieval elite politics, whereas Senji had merely stressed the child's longing for her mother. More important here is how *The Nameless Book* uses the Ippon Princess to bridge the opening comments on the tale and the first three poems of the review, all tied to the Second Princess.

As this arc is considerably more compact than Asukai's story, I will summarize it in its entirety before noting its use by medieval writers. While Sagoromo resolves not to marry the Second Princess, as noted, in book 2, he follows the sound of her *koto* (zither) to her Kokiden apartments at the palace and assaults her,[39] leaving him infatuated but still opposed to a formal relationship; as before, he does not even identify himself, again for fear of precluding a union with the Genji Princess. The snubbed bride conceives his son that night, leading the Saga Empress (*Kōtaigōgū*) to save her daughter's reputation by claiming the baby, only to die of stress upon realizing that the hero is the father but will not admit it. This spurs the Second Princess to take vows, becoming the Cloistered Princess (*Nyūdō no Miya*) and successfully rebuffing Sagoromo thereafter, including during the attempted seduction in

---

38. See Marra, "Part 2," 292; Kuwabara, *Mumyōzōshi*, 59. Since Marra translates *imiji* in various ways, here and below, I generally translate the related excerpts myself. In this passage, Marra prefers "exemplary."

39. This negative characterization is supported by the jarring descriptions of the event, which also vary across texts. For further discussion of both points, see the appendices in Hanna, "The Tale of Sagoromo." For a discussion of the assault in comparative context, see Tonomura, "Coercive Sex in the Medieval Japanese Court," especially 312–13.

Saga. Afterward, he recites a sad poem about whether to pick the area's famous maiden flowers (*ominaeshi*), implying a continued desire for her also seen in his thoughts on the plants' untied "sashes" (*himo*), a trope for overblown blooms that again nods to sex.[40] As I noted in my initial summary of the tale, this ending suggests that he will continue to pursue the Second Princess and his sister, perhaps for another round of the court calendar. Considering the earlier apparition of Asukai's ghost, bound to the world by her own attachments, this structure may even evoke the wheel of karma, with Sagoromo chasing his desires even after death.

Surprisingly, *The Nameless Book* ignores Sagoromo's meeting with the Second Princess, just as it omits the tale's title verse. After the nuns discuss the Ippon Princess, they praise the Second Princess for taking vows, without explaining why she does so. Then they quote the three poems noted earlier: Sagoromo's mournful verse to the Second Princess upon his unwanted marriage; the Saga Emperor's "impressive" reply, evoking his daughter's isolation by describing crickets crying in withered fields; and a poem by the Saga Empress, about the uncertain future of her grandson.[41] This sequence reveals Shunzei's Daughter's lack of interest in the subplot's catalyst as well as her skill in *renga*, with the conversation flowing from topic to topic like the opening sections of the featured commentary and other prefaces by *renga* poets.[42] Like the later remarks on Asukai—who appears earlier in the tale, as noted— this part of the conversation gestures to some of the saddest moments in the Second Princess's arc, but now without letting the heroine speak. Instead, the nuns turn to the Genji Princess, who "seems impressive" (*imijige naru*) but does not suffer enough to warrant further comment;[43] then they turn to

---

40. For Sagoromo's poem and perhaps the most famous example conflating maidenflowers with women, see my notes to the play in chapter 4 (*tachikaeri*; the translation of the other poem, not from the tale, appears in the next note). For an example of the sexual valence of undersashes in particular, see episode 37 of *Ise*, in which the hero specifically asks his lover not to untie these strings in his absence.

41. See Marra, "Part 2," 293; Kuwabara, *Mumyōzōshi*, 59–60. In this case, Marra, too, translates *imiji* as "impressive." Sagoromo's poem to the Second Princess reads as follows: "How could I have dreamed / that I would pass your gate / veiled in trailing plants / and sleep like a traveler / on a pillow of grass?" (*omoiki ya mugura no kado o yukisugite kusa no makura ni tabine semu to wa*). Her father replies: "I imagine that / her old home has gone / completely to ruin, / and become a reed-choked moor / filled with autumn insects' cries" (*furusato wa asajigahara ni narihatete mushi no ne shigeki aki ni zo aramashi*). For the Empress's poem, see the notes to "Sagoromo's Skirts" in chapter 3 (*kumoi made*).

42. On the *renga*-like flow of the prose of a later poet, see Ramirez-Christensen, *Murmured Conversations*, 7.

43. See Marra, "Part 2," 293; Kuwabara, *Mumyōzōshi*, 59. In this passage, Marra translates *imiji* as "quite wonderful." He also interprets the summarized line differently, with the speaker holding that one can sympathize with the Genji Princess despite her self-absorption.

Asukai. The effect is to elide the hero's meeting with the Second Princess and highlight instead the feelings of her parents.

Later writers maintained this selective engagement with the Second Princess's story even when they diverged from the nuns' focus. Only one of the three poems just noted appears in both of the featured collections, for example, and while we cannot infer too much from that given the damage noted below, neither the play nor the other banquet song—both centered on this arc—evokes these poems, either. In fact, only the Asukai-related song even suggests one of them, by alluding to a poem about Asukai's daughter echoed by the Empress's *waka* (both compare Sagoromo's children to pines, contributing to the impression of integration noted earlier). Instead, these tributes tend to consider the Second Princess—when they consider her perspective at all—apart from Sagoromo or the details of their first meeting, even when drawing on their broader relationship.

The play is most obvious here, depicting a courtier who retraces Sagoromo's steps to Saga and meets the heroine's ghost. While the resulting conversation revisits some of her memories of the hero, it also emphasizes clothing, further decentering Senji's narrative by evoking these details in reverse order: first the speakers discuss the ghost's plain, monastic robes, proverbially rotted from tears; then they turn to the colorful garments that she wore in her youth. As that detail suggests, the play cites Sagoromo's poem rejecting her, as well as the Saga Emperor's initial offer of marriage, but neither of those characters appears on stage. Instead, Amewakamiko arrives to banish the Second Princess's tears just after she recalls the hero's performance at the palace, closing the play in an auspicious dance filled with fluttering sleeves and essentially erasing the liaison and her related grief. This ending recalls the banquet song rooted in this arc, which uses references to her sleeves and others to evoke lovers' partings, glossing over her hatred for the hero. Medieval compilers suggest a gentler affair, too, in headnotes that again skirt the details of their first meeting.

Intriguingly, the featured commentary diverges from this softened poetic portrait to mark the subplot's role in Sagoromo's political success. That success involves poetry, too, as medieval writers noticed: while Amaterasu makes the hero emperor in order to protect the imperial line, her priestess (*saigū*) also declares that "the Major Captain is too handsome and talented for this world. It is a shame for him to remain a commoner."[44] This statement portrays Amaterasu as valuing not just birth but also poetic and

---

44. *SNKS* 2:311.

musical talent (*mi no zae*), the very things praised by the gods who appear earlier in the tale, starting with Amewakamiko. While *The Nameless Book* does not mention Amaterasu in its review, the nuns allude to this oracle in their list of unwanted miracles, by objecting that even gifted poets do not cause earthquakes,[45] although this is one of the powers famously assigned to *waka* in *Collection of Ancient and Modern Japanese Poems* (*Kokin wakashū* or *Kokinshū*, ca. 905), the first of the imperial collections noted earlier. In this way, the review acknowledges Senji's pairing of imperial lineage and talent but only to insist on the importance of the former. By contrast, the short narratives stress Sagoromo's gifts, usually noting in the introduction that every woman in the realm—including imperial consorts—desires him, and frequently putting him or his son by Asukai on the throne in the end, without divine intervention. Meanwhile, the featured compilers again glossed over the specifics, gesturing to Sagoromo's imperial rank by noting his final post or using related verbs when quoting his poems but also doing this for other imperial poets, regardless of how they obtained that rank.

Instead, our *renga* master directly underscored the link between Sagoromo's talents and his divinely sanctioned enthronement, by putting sex and genealogy at the head of his guide to the tale. As noted, Senji hinted that Horikawa lost his imperial rank for committing a crime, usually tied in Heian works to acts of lèse majesté. One possibility is that he seduced the hero's mother while she was in service at Amaterasu's shrine, since other tales—notably, *Ise*—evoke similar scandals.[46] Either way, Sagoromo restores his father's line to the palace by an equally flagrant transgression: secretly violating a princess whom the reigning emperor offered to him as a wife. The featured commentary alludes to this event in several ways: notably, by referring to sashes in its title, as detailed below, which connote physical liaisons in addition to recalling the tale's final scene; and by recounting an old story about the Kamo God, involving a historical demoted prince who became emperor. Like other parts of my excerpt, this story underscores the combined role of talent, effort, and blood ties to the throne in the hero's success. In brief, like the short narratives, this tribute hints that even a commoner can rule—perhaps even by unsavory means—as long as he has the gods' support.

Overview of This Book

As will be seen in the chapters, I have attempted to translate allusions to the tale consistently across tributes, at times compromising the flow of the

---

45. For this part of the review, see Marra, "Part 2," 294–95; Kuwabara, *Mumyōzōshi*, 61–63.
46. See episode 69 of *Ise*, in which the hero spends the night with Amaterasu's priestess.

medieval works. While I hope that readers who must rely on my English will not suffer unduly as a result, I have also supplied the Japanese text and short transliterations whenever feasible, so that everyone can appreciate the varying cadences of each work to some degree and specialists can view the libretti in their entirety. My notes expand considerably on the existing annotations and are particularly dense for the commentary. Readers interested in *Sagoromo*'s reception should also consult my appendices, which contain a list of poems useful for finding allusions to the tale elsewhere, as well as short descriptions of alternate texts of the tributes and a list of related secondary sources. While none of these inventories is exhaustive, they provide a good starting point for further research. Here I provide fuller introductions to the featured tributes, focusing on their broader literary and historical connections. Some of this material appears again in the chapters, for ease of reference.

My anthology starts with *The Sagoromo Middle Captain* (*Sagoromo no chūjō*, 1597), in one sense the latest work presented here. Although the cycle reaches back earlier into the medieval era, these short narratives continued to thrive in the early modern period, particularly in illustrated versions, making this work the version of the tale most familiar to later readers.[47] For our purpose, it provides a vivid if loose review of Asukai's story, making it helpful preparation for the next two chapters of this book, which draw from or frequently allude to that subplot.[48] This example from the cycle also contains endearing common touches and captures the broader interest in family and faith seen in medieval literature at large.

Like all of the anonymous writers involved with this cycle, this author or copyist does not appear to have cared for the tale's political thread. While my example depicts Amewakamiko's descent, it also misquotes the poem that inspired Sagoromo's nickname and does not connect these things in the way that Senji suggested. That said, this text also contains a short postscript that resembles the one found in some copies of the tale, praising the emotions experienced and inspired by the characters, albeit with a new emphasis on parents and children.

For our purposes, the more salient detail is the recurring discussion of the boats on which some of the characters travel. In several of the short narratives, including the one presented here, the characters and narrator

---

47. For a discussion of later versions, typically printed and illustrated, see Mashimo, "Kinsei-ki no *Sagoromo no sōshi*."

48. For excerpts from this subplot, see D'Etcheverry, "Story of Sagoromo and Asukai." For an excerpt that introduces book 1 at large, including elements disregarded by medieval writers, see Dutcher, "*Sagoromo*."

repeatedly compare Michinari's fancy vessel with the priest's smaller craft, generating sympathy for the priest (and, by extension, the lovers) while evoking medieval changes in shipbuilding.[49] Since this detail does not advance the plot, it presumably reflects historical developments that the writer found noteworthy. In this respect, one also notes the reference to aristocrats running around in bare feet and the closing comment about social status. While we do not know who wrote or initially read this story, these glimpses of elite jealousy and discomfort reveal more than the common touch praised above. Like Asukai's parents' fear of angering the hero elsewhere in the cycle, such details point to the practical concerns and material lives of the middle aristocracy and of the literate audience writ large.

My second chapter, *Sagoromo: The Wisconsin Collection*, is a new anthology containing the poems used in both *The Genji-Sagoromo Contest* (*Genji Sagoromo awase*, ca. 1206) and the eighteen extant volumes of *Collection of Wind-Blown Leaves* (*Fūyō wakashū*, ca. 1271). The first work constitutes the first half of *Poem Contest in Two Hundred Rounds* (*Monogatari nihyakuban utaawase*), a contest on paper created by Fujiwara Teika (1162–1241), Shunzei's son and Shunzei's Daughter's adoptive brother. The second work, attributed to Teika's son Tameie (1198–1275) and sponsored by Fujiwara Kitsushi (1225–92), a consort of Go-Saga (r. 1242–46), draws solely from fictional tales but mimics the structure of an imperial anthology of verse.

These different formats shaped the compilers' presentation of the tale. Not only did the poetic collection originally contain twenty volumes, like *Collection of Ancient and Modern Japanese Poems*, but the medieval work also contains a similar preface and distributes the tales' poems into the conventional thematic categories, notably longing. Meanwhile, most of Senji's ostensibly seasonal verses appear in the books tied to winter and summer rather than fall and spring, suggesting Senji's independence as a poet but also undercutting her emphasis on the latter, more poetic seasons in the tale's first and last scenes. For the contest, Teika simply matched *Sagoromo*'s poems to the ones he had already chosen from *Genji*, disregarding Senji's narrative in order to illustrate his preferred poetic themes and their treatments.[50] Both compilers also gave *Sagoromo* preferential treatment relative to most other tales, as explained in my introduction to the new set of verse.

---

49. Some examples further distinguish between small, presumably more traditional crafts and large "Chinese boats" (*karabune*). For an overview of changes in the practices of shipwrights over the medieval and early modern periods, see Brooks, "Japanese Wooden Boatbuilding." I am grateful to Wayne Farris for alerting me to the historical significance of this detail.

50. See Vieillard-Baron, "New Worlds."

Critics believe that Kitsushi and her staff, including a niece of Tameie, helped to compile the anthology as well as locate copies of the various tales quoted in it. By presenting the poems from *Sagoromo* that appear in both collections, with these poems restored to their narrative order and grouped by the tale's books, I provide a window into early medieval views of the tale and of the courtly past more generally, as recalled by the elite poets who preserved and disseminated it. Tellingly, their shared selections emphasize longing, particularly his feelings for Asukai. My *Wisconsin Collection* thus includes twenty-seven poems by Sagoromo, compared to six by Asukai and four by the Second Princess, with over a third of his verses tied to the first heroine. This emphasis on the hero contrasts sharply with the selections from the tale in *The Nameless Book*, composed (as noted) by Teika's foster sister and Tameie's "aunt."

At the same time, the persistent focus on Asukai, in one way or another—given the material difficulties that mark this subplot—seems to echo the concerns of an increasingly financially constrained elite. By contrast, Teika and Tameie (or perhaps Kitsushi) appear to have had little interest in the Genji Princess, with my selection containing just two of her poems (if also a number of the hero's verses about her). While we cannot be certain, given the damage to the later anthology, this impression again recalls Shunzei's Daughter, who gave this heroine's lack of suffering as a reason for not discussing her further in *The Nameless Book*.

In general, my *Wisconsin Collection* shows that medieval poets skillfully highlighted the more appealing poetic portraits of the court, unsurprising in an era that produced a *New Collection of Ancient and Modern Japanese Poems* (*Shin Kokinshū*, ca. 1205)—compiled in part by Teika. Kitsushi's son Go-Fukakusa (r. 1246–60) even organized a reenactment of a splendid fictional concert from *The Tale of Genji*.[51] In the same way, the competing headnotes seen in my collection edit out presumably distasteful details crucial to Senji's narrative, instead identifying the tale with beautiful portraits of sorrow that served the compilers' own didactic needs and interests.

My third chapter presents the banquet songs "*Sagoromo's Sleeves*" (*Sagoromo no sode*) and "*Sagoromo's Skirts*" (*Sagoromo no tsuma*), titles that create poetic series of words (*engo*) about garments; the titles can also be read as "The Robe's Sleeves" and "The Robe's Skirts," or "The Narrow Robe's Sleeves" and so forth. The second title also puns on "*Sagoromo's Spouse*" via a so-called pivot word (*kakekotoba*), another technique popular in verse. These

---

51. This event is described in book 3 of *An Unsolicited Tale* (*Towazugatari*, after 1306), translated by Karen Brazell as *The Confessions of Lady Nijō*.

libretti come from *Treatise on Banquet Songs* (*Enkyokushō*, 1301), one of the first anthologies compiled by the art's founder Myōkū or Meigū (n.d.). Other pronunciations of his name are possible; all we know for certain about him, other than his leading role in this obscure genre, is that he lived in or near Kamakura and that he started compiling the art during the tenure of the eighth shogun, Prince Hisaaki or Hisaakira (in office 1289–1308).

Hisaaki was the child of Emperor Go-Fukakusa, noted above, illustrating how court culture radiated out from Kyoto in the early medieval period to shape cultural life in Kamakura. Indeed, our record of Go-Fukakusa's *Genji*-themed concert comes from a woman who traveled to Kamakura herself, advising the new shogun's attendants on courtly furnishings and dress.[52] Myōkū's anthologies, meanwhile, contain libretti ascribed to Tameie's brother and to his mother, Teika's widow Abutsu (ca. 1222–83), another famous visitor to Kamakura who also reportedly copied *Sagoromo* itself.[53]

More important for our purposes, Myōkū wrote and scored both of the songs featured here, signaling his special interest in *Sagoromo* (even *Genji* only inspired one song) and his art's distinct concerns. While such works were performed by men and often treat religious or martial topics, these particular libretti shift among the perspectives of Sagoromo and his lovers, favoring the Second Princess and Asukai and reversing the narrative order of emphasis: "Sleeves" relies largely on material from the subplot concerning the former, while "Skirts" depends heavily on the lines tied to the latter.

As noted, the songs also seem designed to merge in performance,[54] further eliding the content and narrative relationship of the two arcs from the tale. Sung first, "Sleeves" emphasizes lovers' partings, leading listeners to interpret "Skirts" as stressing sorrows of travel and effectively creating a longer song about leaving both people and places behind. Both are common themes in Myōkū's libretti, which often describe the road from the imperial capital to Kamakura, a route familiar to men like Hisaaki, who arrived at his post as a young teenager. In *Treatise on Banquet Songs*, my examples sit between songs about writing brushes and hawks, further integrating them into the lives of their singers and audience.

Intriguingly, these libretti and Myōkū's anthologies in general exhibit an associative flow familiar from *renga* and the other poetic influences foregrounded

---

52. See book 4 of *An Unsolicited Tale*.
53. See Sudō, *Sagoromo monogatari juyō no kenkyū*, chap. 3, for a discussion of a fragment of the manuscript in question, also attributed to Abutsu's son Tamesuke (1263–1328).
54. See Tonomura, "Sōka ni okeru monogatari-kayōka no hōhō."

in his first preface, which includes allusions to Tameie's relatives.[55] While this flowing style tends to undermine narrative concerns, as noted in my discussion of *The Nameless Book*, it also creates a powerful sense of immediacy: not just because the shifting focal points compel close attention, as in a *renga* sequence (or in conversation, as Shunzei's Daughter demonstrated), but also because the shared experience of live performance presumably also generated a sense of community for singers and audience alike.

Perhaps as a result, Myōkū's students continued to copy the anthologies and perform them for warrior houses, including in Kyoto, until the end of the medieval period. Oda Hidenobu (1580–1605), the grandson of warlord Oda Nobunaga (1534–82), even deposited a copy of one of Myōkū's anthologies, complete with secret teachings, at the family temple on the eve of the battle that essentially ended the medieval era, suggesting the longevity and importance of banquet song as a medieval art.[56] While the *Sagoromo*-inspired libretti were not in Hidenobu's book, this event also underscores how the tale and other Heian works became important to the descendants of men whom courtly writers like Senji arguably mocked.[57] Like Tameie and Teika, these medieval warriors and their noble associates broke *Sagoromo* into pieces, in this case to create sympathetic portraits of their own lives, physically and socially divorced from the imperial palace.

My fourth chapter returns us to Kyoto, if not the palace, with the Noh play *Sagoromo* (ca. 1503), translated here as *Sagoromo: Narrow Robes* to highlight its focus on garments and related financial constraints. The libretto was written by courtier and scholar Sanjōnishi Sanetaka (1455–1537), the author of the genealogy of the tale's characters noted earlier and the most famous member of the family that recorded early commentaries on the tale in their copies of its text. Perhaps for that reason, shogun Ashikaga Yoshihisa (in office 1473–89) requested Sanetaka to write this play, at least according to the noble's diary entry from 1481.[58] Playwright Kanze Nobumitsu (1435–1516) later scored and choreographed Sanetaka's libretto and, after consulting with him on how to sing it, staged it twice at the shogun's palace in 1503,

---

55. See the text in *SZ*, 27–29. There is also a useful list of song titles, separated by anthology, followed by a preface to later anthologies, on 29–39.

56. See the introduction to *SZ*, 3–11. I refer to the Battle of Sekigahara in 1600, which set the stage for the Tokugawa shogunate.

57. The portrait of the uncouth warrior who attempts to add Tamakazura to his collection of wives in *The Tale of Genji* is a famous example, even though it also provides an ironic counterpoint to the actions of Genji himself. In *Sagoromo*, one thinks of the Asukai subplot, in which the nurse not only tries to marry her charge to Michinari (whose rough warrior escort frightens Asukai) but threatens to run off with a coarse eastern general herself.

58. See McCormick, *Tosa Mitsunobu*, 106.

presumably for shogun Ashikaga Yoshizumi (in office 1495–1508).[59] Since Yoshizumi was indebted to the Hosokawa family for his position, and they like the other great warrior houses enjoyed banquet song,[60] perhaps he or his sponsors had heard and liked Myōkū's libretti. Banquet song in general exerted a strong influence on Noh, by this time the dominant performing art.

Meanwhile, Sanetaka—who clearly knew the tale's plot, given his chart—used the structure of a ghost play to recall a glorious past, sidestepping inconvenient details like the Second Princess's hatred for the hero just like the earlier song and poetic collections and reversing the subplot's grim conclusion to create the fantasy centered on elegant clothing discussed earlier. Sanetaka pawned his own robes at least once to supplement his finances, leaving him unable to attend an event at the palace and suggesting a personal stake in the play's sartorial focus.[61]

However, as my notes to the translation suggest, Sanetaka's libretto also continues many allusions also seen in *"Sagoromo's Sleeves,"* raising the possibility that he, if not Yoshizumi, knew Myōkū's work. Indeed, Sanetaka also apparently wrote a lost play called *Tokiwa*, a "poem-pillow" or poetic site (*utamakura*) tied to loyalty but also the name of the hill where Asukai dies; four related verses appear in my *Wisconsin Collection*.[62] Given the medieval influence of my sources there, it seems plausible that the missing libretto drew on Asukai's story and perhaps even *"Sagoromo's Skirts"* to reproduce Myōkū's attention to both of the tale's most popular arcs. Regardless, Sanetaka's extant libretto suggests the tale's value to late medieval elites, as a symbol of glories they hoped to bring back.

The final selection in my anthology comes from the commentary *Sagoromo's Undersash* (*Sagoromo no shitahimo*, ca. 1590), often just labeled *Undersash*; author Satomura Jōha (1524–1602) himself uses that shorter title in his first sentence.[63] As noted, this *renga* master had particularly strong connections to the late medieval era's upstart warrior houses, instructing both Oda Nobunaga and his successor Toyotomi Hideyoshi (1537–98), who famously suspected Jōha (for a time) of being involved in Nobunaga's death.[64]

---

59. On Nobumitsu and the performances, see Lim, *Another Stage*, 40–41 and 182.

60. See *SZ*, 10.

61. See Horton, "Portrait of a Medieval Japanese Marriage," 136.

62. See poems 27, 32, 33, and 41 in chapter 2 (*aki no iro wa, koto no ha o, nao tanomu*, and *nagaraete*).

63. This translation of the title revises my earlier version of it, in order to foreground Jōha's gesture to layers of meaning, discussed below. For the earlier translation, in an aside discussing Jōha's response to Asukai's wetnurse, see D'Etcheverry, "Out of the Mouths of Nurses," 159. As seen there, *himo* literally refer to strings, but "sash" sounds more suggestive in English.

64. See Okuda, *Rengashi*, chap. 5. Intriguingly, this story involves Jōha rescuing a prince from Nobunaga's company just before the assassination took place. As Okuda also details, the *renga* master

Critics suggest that Jōha wrote *Undersash* for Hideyoshi or then-heir Hidetsugu (1568–95); the preface evokes the Toyotomi by invoking Nagara Bridge, located near their castle,[65] and Hideyoshi became regent the year that Jōha finished his initial draft. One imagines the tale's political arc appealed to Hideyoshi, who also prevailed on the court to make Hidetsugu regent after him, despite their decidedly common birth.

That said, the Toyotomi and other late medieval warriors did not rely exclusively on force to achieve their ends, something that Jōha's preface to *Undersash* also suggests. In addition to suggesting Hideyoshi's fortress, Nagara Bridge is another *utamakura* for longevity, invoked in the preface to *Collection of Wind-Blown Leaves* and associated with the emperor whose wife sponsored it (see chapter 5). As a poet who also wrote commentaries on famous anthologies of verse as well as on *Genji* and *Ise*, Jōha must have been aware of that fact. Indeed, the preface pointedly evokes the anthology of tale-verse by noting the many tales gathered by that bridge, connecting his efforts (and Hideyoshi's regency) to the courtly past.

As stated earlier, Jōha also complained that those copies contained errors, forcing him to collate texts of *Sagoromo*. Sanetaka's chart of characters, also mentioned in the preface (along with the names of two other famous scholars and poets), could not provide enough help because, like other medieval writers, the *renga* master did not focus on Senji's characters or plot. Instead, his glosses generally clarify the meanings of various words, poems, and intertexts, although the glosses, too, became jumbled over time. Since Jōha loaned out his draft as he revised it, *Undersash* has several textual lineages, and not simply because of the tale's shifting corpus.[66]

To the best of my knowledge, every version contained the preface, genealogical charts, and discursive genealogies translated here, followed by over a thousand glosses keyed to Jōha's lost copy of *Sagoromo* and presented in narrative order, sorted by the tale's four books. In general, book 1 receives the most glosses; otherwise, the later the copy, the greater the total number of glosses, as Jōha and then his students added to his work. Along with the front matter, I present the first hundred glosses from my text of *Undersash*, which start with short excerpts from the tale and collectively bring us to the night of Sagoromo's fateful concert in book 1.

Despite the disruptive effect of my extensive notes, the preface and discursive passages within the genealogical section feature a notably poetic style,

---

again incurred Hideyoshi's displeasure by association years later, when the warlord turned on Hidetsugu, forcing Jōha into exile.

65. See Ueno, "Jōha no baai," 474.
66. See the discussion in *SMKR*, 3–12.

flowing from topic to topic in a fashion that recalls other treatises by *renga* poets, as well as *The Nameless Book* and Myōkū's anthologies. As my readers will have noticed, Jōha's title evokes another poetic series of terms about garments ("robes" and "undersash") as well as hidden layers of meaning, here tied to the Second Princess. If one "unties" (*toku*) a sash, as seen in my earlier discussion of the tale's conclusion, medieval writers used the same verb to describe solving riddles (*nazo*), here linked to *Genji* and the "heart" (*kokoro*) of *Sagoromo*—another poetic term, this time for a work's essence.

While I do not have the space to analyze *Undersash* here, this reference to inner truths seems bound up with Jōha's genealogical charts, which feature historical emperors and courtiers, drawing attention to the tale's political thread just like the opening nod to sashes and, thus, the tale's conclusion—with Sagoromo on the throne, even if he cannot get what he really wants. Jōha's preface credits his punning title to the Kamo God, who allegedly left the paper for *Undersash* pretitled at the bottom of a box of the Nirvana Sutra—that is, beneath a valuable layer of teachings and thus presumably important. In this way, the *renga* master performed a fascinating interpretive about-face, using a tale once synonymous with longing and courtly glory to find secret meaning in Sagoromo's assault of the Princess. This conclusion echoes his debts to Jien (1155–1225), an early medieval historian cited in my notes to the translation known for his apologist's view of Fujiwara control of the throne.[67]

Here a short postscript to my medieval story seems in order. While Hideyoshi failed to unite and rule Japan, the family later worshipped him as a god, recalling the deification of Sagoromo in the short narratives still circulating in that era. Meanwhile, the Tokugawa clan, initially Hideyoshi's allies, brought his plan to partial fruition, by taking practical control of the realm and then forcing the court to accept a Tokugawa empress, whose first daughter became the first female sovereign in over eight hundred years.[68] Intriguingly, the first printing of *Sagoromo* appeared in 1623, just three years after that marriage. Meanwhile, another printing appeared in 1654, which included a text of *Undersash*, Sanetaka's genealogy of characters, a chronology of the tale's events, and numerous pictures of well-dressed courtiers,

---

67. See Hambrick, "The *Gukanshō*," and the introduction to Brown and Ishida, *The Future and the Past*.

68. That is, Tokugawa Masako (1607–78), who married Go-Mizunoo (1596–1680) in 1620. On both clans' ambitions and their founders' alleged divinity, which also recalls Nobunaga, see Boot, "The Death of a Shogun." On the Tokugawa's struggle to get their bloodline on the throne, see Tanaka, *Kiku to aoi*. As Tanaka observes, their victory was ultimately pyrrhic, since the female sovereign noted below did not marry and therefore could not produce an heir.

testifying to how Kyoto's finances improved with Tokugawa support. Like the rest of the tale's visual and early modern reception, that story lies beyond the scope of this book. However, those pictures present a poignant reminder of Sanetaka's practical concerns, just as the print on the cover of this book—which, in its full form, contains poems—recalls the enduring poetic engagement with Senji's tale.

Put broadly, this anthology of medieval works confirms more than *The Tale of Sagoromo*'s role as a flexible symbol for literate Japanese in the twelfth through sixteenth centuries. As my summaries suggest, and the ensuing translations illustrate in detail, medieval writers used Senji's work in very different ways, despite their literary and historical connections, to confront different challenges and opportunities. Their works thus present a wide range of responses to the tale and to change in general, refracted through shared materials but gesturing to the diversity of their experiences and aspirations. We can also discern a pattern, based on their shared extracts from the tale. Whatever their interests or circumstances, these writers generally cited the same painful events from a tale that also features joyful and comic elements. Whether they did so to teach poetry, forge social bonds, underscore the power of the gods, or hint at paths to political success, they celebrated sorrow through *Sagoromo* and, in the process, made their own dreams and disappointments relevant to a broader audience. In short, they wove their lives into Senji's work. It is to their words—written with new hearts, as Shunzei and Teika might have put it[69]—that we turn next.

---

69. Both poets proclaimed that *waka* ideally combined old words and new hearts: that is, allusions in the service of new sentiments and effects. See the entry on *kokoro* in the glossary to Carter, *How to Read a Japanese Poem*. While I had not intended to draw any allusions when I chose my title, Margaret H. Childs's study and translations of four unrelated medieval tales, *Rethinking Sorrow*, also resonates here. As those works demonstrate, other medieval writers put the theme of sorrow to new uses, too; something also seen in *Sagoromo*'s tributes.

Chapter 1

The Sagoromo Middle Captain

Overview

As detailed in my introduction, this short narrative belongs to a cycle of late medieval and early modern works that revisit *The Tale of Sagoromo*, giving the hero and Asukai a happy ending. Many of these anonymous works use the same or similar titles, highlighting the hero's sobriquet and early posts in the tale. They also exhibit a common touch particularly pronounced in this example and many poems not found in modern editions of the tale. Not all of them appear in the cycle's other lineages, although whether they are new to my example is hard to say.

My base text appears in Yokoyama Shigeru's *Muromachi jidai monogatari*. It transcribes the Keichō 2 (1597) manuscript held by Keiō Gijuku University Library, notable for its extensive pronunciation guides. The same transcription appears in Yokoyama's collaboration with Matsumoto Ryūshin, *Muromachi jidai monogatari taisei*, which provides a helpful introduction to the cycle, while Nakano Kōichi's *Nara ehon emakishū* presents a photographed version of a similar illustrated text. While I do not include any of those pictures here, I do try to convey the popular flavor of the prose in this example, by preserving the somewhat choppy and often conversational flow of the narration. I also generally reproduce redundant passages and the use of alternate names for the same character, since they not unduly impede the flow of the story and suggest the author's or copyist's interests.

Translation

Long ago on our Dragonfly Island of Japan, perhaps during the reign of Emperor Kammu, there lived a court minister.[1] His son, known as the Sagoromo Middle Captain, was strikingly handsome and a talented musician and poet. Whether it was Japanese or Chinese verse, or anything else, Sagoromo stood in a class by himself.[2] As a result, the court treated him as its greatest treasure, and every woman who saw him, regardless of rank, lost her heart. Even imperial consorts scorned their positions, feeling that only the love of someone like Sagoromo could make life worth living.[3] Calling him splendid hardly does him justice.

Sagoromo got his nickname when he was fifteen, during a visit to the palace. It was the thirteenth night of the Ninth Month, and the moon shone unclouded in the sky. After singing some Chinese verse, he took up his flute, and even people not usually moved by music felt their sins lighten just listening to him. As if sharing their admiration, a heavenly being appeared and presented the boy with his feathered robe.[4] Looking still more handsome, the boy recited the following verse:

色々にそでははかさねて人しれずおもひそめてし夜わのさごろも

One color atop	*iro iro ni*
other sleeves now overlapped;	*sode wa kasanete*
though I hide the truth,	*hito shirezu*
it already bears love's hue,	*omoisometeshi*
this narrow robe worn at night.[5]	*yowa no sagoromo*

It was because of this verse that people called him Sagoromo. Thirty-one different families, from senior nobles to men of mean estate, offered Sagoromo

---

1. Kammu reigned from 781 to 806. Other tales in the cycle date the story to different reigns, among other variations.

2. The narrator puns on *naniwa no koto*, which means "everything" but suggests Naniwa (Osaka) and, by extension, the *naniwazu* poem from the preface of *Collection of Ancient and Modern Japanese Poems*. That verse was used to teach children poetry.

3. The narrator comments more specifically on the evils of human birth. I have omitted a similar line about the consorts driving themselves to distraction over the hero.

4. Strictly speaking, the text only has a heavenly being (*tennin*) taking the robe off. I have supplied the detail from the tale and used it to explain why the hero looks "still more handsome" in the next line.

5. This version of the poem differs significantly from those included in the three versions of the tale considered here in that it omits the hero's vow to sleep alone. That verse, which also begins *iro iro ni*, is translated in my introduction from the text found in *SNKS*. It also appears in *NKBT* (52) and, with a minor variation in the last line, in *SNKZ* (1:54).

their daughters in marriage.[6] When he wouldn't so much as look at the women, several of them died of disappointment.

Then Sagoromo turned twenty-one. On the second night of the Second Month, coming home from the palace, he came across a Mount Ōhara carriage near Awataguchi.[7] He could just see a priest's robe trailing out from beneath the long blinds. "That's odd," Sagoromo thought to himself. "Why would a priest use a woman's carriage?" When he asked the members of his escort to investigate, they looked through the blinds and reported that a priest was inside—with a woman. "I knew it," thought Sagoromo. He told his men to have the priest step into the street.[8]

"What kind of a priest rides around with a woman?" They shouted through the blinds. "Come out here right now. If you don't, we've got orders to pull you out ourselves." At this the priest, apparently frightened, jumped out and ran off, and Sagoromo's men had to content themselves with interrogating his servant.[9] "Who was that?" they demanded.

"He's someone important from Kiyomizu,"[10] the man answered. "As for what he was doing here, well, he somehow caught a glimpse of this lady and became obsessed, so he stole her from Uzumasa, where she'd been on retreat."[11] The servant told them everything.

Satisfied, the members of the escort chased him off, too, with a warning. "We weren't going to let you go, but since you told us the truth, you saved your life."

Next Sagoromo climbed into the carriage to speak with the woman, who was as lovely as the autumn moon and even more graceful than a wild cherry tree.[12] As she lay there in tears, incomparably beautiful, his heart went out to her. "What should I do?" he asked gently, and when she ignored him, he hesitated further. If he embarrassed her, would she speak? He tried pleading with

---

6. "Senior nobles" glosses *kugyō tenjōbito*. The first half of the phrase generally refers to courtiers of the fifth rank and higher, the court elite. Their sons would also be high ranked.

7. *Ōhara yama no kuruma*. I am unable to identify this kind of carriage, other than to reiterate the obvious association with Ōhara. This region, to the north of the city, was famous for its hermitages; this suggests the priest. Ōhara was also known for its female peddlers, who brought brushwood to the capital on their heads. The label may thus suggest Asukai. Sagoromo's own reference to a woman's carriage (*onnaguruma*) echoes the tale. Awataguchi was on the eastern side of the city.

8. Sagoromo has with him two kinds of retainers: *zuijin* (members of the palace guard who provided an armed escort for high-ranking nobles), and *zōshiki* (more general servants).

9. *Kotei warare* (presumably a mistake for *warawa*). A low-ranking servant of indeterminate age. The tale specifies an oxherd.

10. Kiyomizu Temple, also located on the eastern side of the city.

11. Uzumasa was home to Kōryūji, a Shingon temple said to house an image of the Buddha carved by Prince Shōtoku. Like most of the scene, this detail comes from the tale.

12. *Sanka ni chiru hana*. Literally, "a blossom that falls in the mountains and rivers."

her, but she still remained silent, until he thought that even a stone would break first.[13] "It appears that there is nothing I can do," he said at last. "You must miss that priest who brought you here, even if he did run out on you. Don't worry, you will probably see him again somewhere. I will go now."

Stung by this remark, the woman raised her head slightly and saw that he was not just anyone.[14] She spoke up, apparently reassured. "What is there to hide? I was on retreat at Uzumasa, when a carriage came for me with the message that my mother had fallen ill. I got in immediately, but once we were underway that priest joined me and confessed that the story about my mother was a lie and that he was taking me away somewhere. I wanted to die. And then to be seen like this. . . ." She spoke in a whisper, clearly embarrassed.

Moved, Sagoromo tried to console her. "I can only have found you because we share a bond from another life," he insisted. He pledged his love for her right there in the street, but she just kept crying and asking to go home, so he asked her where that was and offered to take her there. "After all," he pointed out, "people will find it strange if we stay here like this."

Overjoyed by Sagoromo's offer, she told him her name, although she hadn't intended to do so.

あすかひの水にやどれる月なればくもりありとはたれか見るべき

Since it is the moon	Asukai no
that rests in the waters	mizu ni yadoreru
here at Asukai,	tsuki nareba
who would speak of clouds and hide	kumori ari to wa
my name from you as you suggest?[15]	tare ka mirubeki

At this, Sagoromo realized that she was Asukai, the daughter of the Governor-General Middle Counselor who lived on West Tōin near Nijō.[16]

---

13. *Ikanaru iwaki nari to mo, kore hodo ni, kataku wa araji.* Literally, "even boulders and trees wouldn't be that hard."

14. *Yo no tsune no hito ni te wa owasezarikereba.* She instinctively gives him an honorific verb, although what prompts this response is unclear. Perhaps it was his robes, since he was returning from court.

15. "Since you are clearly someone important, no one will blame me for asking your help. I live at Asukai." In the tale, Asukai and Sagoromo exchange poems using the same toponym, a famous spring discussed in my introduction. See the notes to "Sagoromo's Skirts" in chapter 3 (*tomare to mo* and *Asukai ni*).

16. *Sotsu no chūnagon.* The post of *sotsu* or *sochi*, head of the imperial outpost of Dazaifu in Kyushu, was nominally filled by a prince. Distance made this hardship duty, and most appointees, like Asukai's father, sent deputies in their place.

As they rode along they continued to talk. "I know what you're thinking," said Sagoromo. "Since you're so fond of that priest, you probably can't wait to see him tonight and discuss your adventures. I ought to come by and listen to the lies you'll tell him about me."

"Please come and judge the truth for yourself," she parried.

"Tonight, then." With this, he left.

Asukai's parents were astonished to see her back from her retreat so early.[17] She brushed off their questions by saying that she had come down with a cold and borrowed a carriage from her uncle. Her mother was particularly happy to see her.[18] Meanwhile, all Sagoromo could think of was sunset. If only it would come early! Finally, at dusk, he stole away to Asukai's house.[19]

There he found a gap in the standing screens and saw her facing her brazier, drawing in the spent ashes.[20] Her profile was so dazzling in the lamplight that calling it splendid hardly does her justice. When night fell, he slipped inside to see her and found her still harder to part with. When the lady asked his name, his reply was as follows:

ふぢごろも きたる身なれば かくれなし おりけむ人をたれととへかし

As I am someone	fujigoromo
who wears wisteria robes	kitaru mi nareba
there's nowhere to hide;	kakure nashi
perhaps it is the weaver's name	orikemu hito o
that you ought to ask about.[21]	tare to toekashi

---

17. The narrator does not specify whose parents these are. While the context makes this clear, it should still surprise readers of the court tale. There Asukai is an orphan, whose father held the post noted above.

18. The narrator gives no reason why this should be so.

19. The narrator describes her home as a *gosho*, a residence belonging to someone wealthy or of high rank. This is another significant change from the tale, in which the orphaned heroine lives with her wetnurse at a cheap residence.

20. *Haikaki shitamaite zo owashikeru.* Alternatively, she may be cleaning out the ashes, but this seems a menial task for the daughter of a noble of this rank. Such work would evoke the tale; there, Asukai's poverty fascinates the hero.

21. "My robes give me away. You should ask yourself who inspired this deep passion. It was you." Wisteria robes (*fujigoromo*) were rough, originally woven from vines. Since the term also names mourning robes, Sagoromo may imply that he mourns in Asukai's absence, foreshadowing her death. The poem also recalls the court tale: in particular, Sagoromo's first, ambiguous response to the offer of the Second Princess. There he tells the Saga Emperor that, "If it were lavender, / that personal substitute-robe, / then—if it were that— / it would certainly surpass / the sleeves of that heavenly maid" (*murasaki no mi no shiro goromo sore naraba otome no sode ni masari koso seme*). The poem blurs the Princess's sleeves with Amewakamiko's robes, as my somewhat loose translation suggests. The reference to "lavender," meanwhile, evokes the Genji Princess, with whom Sagoromo has a poetically related family tie; see the notes to "Sagoromo's Sleeves" in chapter 3 for an explanation

Asukai could not understand what he meant by "wisteria robes." According to one commentary, wisteria robes were robes worn by mourners.[22] There was also a poem that someone composed after being criticized for riding past the Kamo Shrine instead of getting out of his carriage first.

ふぢごろもきたる身なればおそれなしおりよとおもふ神はあらじな

As I am someone	fujigoromo
who wears wisteria robes	kitaru mi nareba
there's nothing to fear;	osore nashi
there can be no god who would	oriyo to omou
command me to dismount.	kami wa arajina

The words were the same, but she had no idea what he meant. However, since it would have been embarrassing to ask, she pretended to understand, never dreaming that her visitor was Sagoromo.

"Being with you is like being in another world," he sighed. "May you never hate me in this one."[23]

"Why would I hate you?" she answered fondly, and the night passed quickly in such banter, with no time to dream. Then came the rooster's cry announcing the dawn.[24] While they must have been grieved at this parting, theirs was a secret affair and Sagoromo left, promising to return at sunset.[25]

From then on, they were together every night. As time passed, Asukai conceived a child, but the affair was too secret for her to think of telling her parents. Nor did Sagoromo want the wife that his parents had chosen for him to find out, although he loved Asukai dearly. As the lovers grew closer and

---

of this metaphor, made famous by *The Tale of Genji*. In the present verse, the reference to "wisteria" evokes "lavender," both as related colors and via the same passage in *Genji*.

22. *Keseu chū*. I have not been able to identify this.

23. *Nikushi to oboshimesunayo*. This seems a non sequitur, but it does foreshadow later events. As noted in the introduction to the present volume, Asukai dies without seeing Sagoromo again. Her diary from her final years expresses both her longing for him and some resentment at his failure to find her. The line noted here is presumably another example of the writer assuming knowledge of the tale, since there the hero has a chance to bring Asukai home but fails to do so.

24. *Yagoe no tori* ("the eight-cry bird"), so-called because its repeated call is so jarring, particularly to lovers' ears.

25. This is a fascinating passage. First the narrator invites the reader to imagine the lovers' feelings, perhaps in response to an illustration. Then, he explains why the pair must ignore their emotions: literally, "because theirs was a relationship that avoided people's eyes" (*hitome o tsutsumitamau on'naka*). The narrator repeats this point a few lines later. This may be because, as we learn later, Sagoromo already has a wife. I have chosen a broader explanation, one consistent with the traditional fictional division between political marriages and clandestine romance. In the tale, interestingly, Sagoromo avoids discovery for another reason: his secret passion for his foster sister, from whom he wishes to hide the affair.

he continued to hesitate, Sagoromo was named Senior Assistant Governor-General of Tsukushi.[26]

When the new major captain got home from the palace, his delighted father told him the news.[27] "That's wonderful! Now, how shall we handle this?[28] Your wetnurse's son is the Senior Assistant Minister in the Palace Guards.[29] Let's send him as your replacement." Sagoromo agreed, and they chose the twelfth day of the Eleventh Month for his retainer's departure. The Assistant Minister's parents were ecstatic about his promotion. "You can't take your master's place in Tsukushi without a wife,"[30] they pointed out. As they were searching for a suitable person, someone mentioned Asukai, the daughter of the Governor-General Middle Counselor who lived on West Tōin near Nijō; apparently, she wasn't married yet. The man's parents sent a letter to the Governor-General's wife on the spot.

When his wife told him about the proposal, the Governor-General immediately agreed: "I hate to send our only daughter so far away, but if we don't get her settled before we die, who will look after her? Since this man seems to be doing well, I have no objections." His wife sent a favorable reply, and the date was set. Soon it was the night before Asukai's departure. When her parents called her to them and gave her the news, she burst into tears. "They don't know that I met someone!" she realized. "What should I do?"

"Why are you carrying on like this about leaving home?" her mother demanded.

"I don't want to leave you and father," Asukai hedged. "Tsukushi is so far away."

"I know," her mother sighed. "We have so few children that I wish I could keep you with us forever, but seeing you settled now will keep us from worrying about you when we're dead. And it's not like he's just anyone. His mother was wetnurse to the famous Sagoromo Middle Captain, and he's the Senior Assistant Minister in the Palace Guards. Not just anyone could take his master's place in Tsukushi. You may not want to go so far away, but this

---

26. *Daini.* The first clause is my best guess at the phrase: "*shizen, nushi mogana to omoiawasete.*" Ironically, Sagoromo has been appointed to go to Dazaifu in her father's place.

27. This passage is confusing, since it must refer to either the hero or his father—both of whom currently hold other posts. I have translated as if the hero has just been promoted, to go with his named promotion, but after this the narrator resumes calling him by his old office of middle captain.

28. This translation is rather free. The line literally reads *Jiki ni wa, ikaga sen* ("What shall we do first?"). Since the narrator doesn't mention any second steps, I amended the line to make the passage read more smoothly.

29. *Hyōe no Taifu.*

30. *Daikan ni genin wa yamame ni te wa kudarazaru mono to te.* The reasoning here is unclear. They may fear that he won't meet someone suitable in what was essentially an international port.

is a wonderful chance for you. Don't be so upset." Nonetheless, Asukai was weeping so hard that she withdrew to her room in embarrassment.

There she began to worry about what her secretive lover would think. She already hated being parted from him, finding even the daily wait until sunset almost unbearable and now, uncertain what to do, she nearly choked on her tears. Then something even worse occurred to her. What if, for some strange reason, he didn't come that night? Struggling to think of something to leave him to remember her by, she decided on a letter. You can imagine her misery as she wrote.

Sagoromo, meanwhile, had been missing Asukai more than ever. If only the sun would set early for once! He waited impatiently, eager to see her again and talk over the day's events. When night fell, he hurried over, only to find her looking as if she'd been crying all day: she just lay there in tears, speechless.

He rushed to her side, heart pounding. "What's wrong? You look terrible, but no matter what's bothering you, there's no need to dwell on it like this. What happened? Did your parents find out about us and get angry with you? If that's it, don't worry. Tomorrow I'll send my wife away and bring you home with me. Then nothing will come between us. Just please don't cry like that."

This only made Asukai more miserable, and she wouldn't even look at him. "If only I could tell him the truth!" she thought. But he was sure to find out in any case, and what would he think of her tomorrow, when he heard what had happened? Mortified, she could not bring herself to explain anything, and when he continued to press her, she finally muttered irritably that he should be able to figure it out.

Sagoromo grew more and more agitated. Could she be dying? He resolved to bring her home with him on the very next night, reasoning that nothing too bad could happen during daylight,[31] and for the rest of the night, he tried to cheer her up, while she pretended that nothing was wrong. When dawn came—the sound of the birds urging him to leave broke their hearts—and Sagoromo started to get ready to go, Asukai broke down again. Would she ever see him now, even in her dreams? Blinded by tears, she clung to his sleeve, the very picture of grief.

By now Sagoromo was extremely worried, but all he could do was to repeat that he would come for her that night and so, urging her to dry her tears and wait for sunset, he left. Her weeping image stayed with him all the

---

31. *Hiru no hodo ni nani no koto no arubeki zo.* Sagoromo's expectations seem formed by suspicion or by court fiction, where tragedy often strikes at night. The present work's more realistic catastrophe (departure for a forced marriage) occurs in daylight.

way home.[32] Hurrying inside, he sent his wife away, then had rooms prepared for Asukai.

The Assistant Minister arrived in the midst of the hustle and bustle to take his leave. "Everything's ready," he reported. "I've come to say goodbye."

"But you haven't been here at all lately,"[33] Sagoromo objected. The Assistant Minister offered to put off the trip until the morning, but since this was the only good day for it, Sagoromo urged him not to wait.[34] "Take this fan as a parting gift," he said. "It's inscribed by someone I've grown very close to recently. We wrote poems together in honor of that bright moon on the fifteenth of the Eighth Month, and hers is on one side. I normally wouldn't dream of parting with this, but I will give it to you as a token of our friendship. May it bring you luck."[35]

After taking his leave, the Assistant Minister went straight to the Yodo River to meet his boat.[36] Meanwhile, at the Counselor's house, a carriage had come for Asukai, shortly after Sagoromo left. Her parents presented her with a beautiful set of robes. "Don't act like a child," they scolded her. "Remember, you don't have a choice." Asukai put the robes on as she was, without even doing her makeup, which angered her mother; she left in a huff. Meanwhile, Asukai wondered what taking her lover's carriage later that night would have felt like.[37]

Calling over an attendant she trusted, who had known about the affair from the beginning, Asukai handed her the letter that she had written. "Please don't tell him that I've gone to Tsukushi," she instructed the woman. "I'd hate for him to know that I hid that from him." Then, since they were in a hurry, she climbed into the carriage, which took her to someplace called Yodo, a port. Back home, the attendant to whom she'd entrusted the letter wailed loudly with the rest of Asukai's servants, wishing that they could have gone with her.

---

32. *Michisugara, shitaitamau omokage, mi ni sou kokochi shite.* The line evokes Genji's trip to Suma.

33. *Kono higoro aware kore e mukaete misezaritsuru netasa yo.* Since the Assistant Minister claims that Sagoromo told him about his plans to bring Asukai home that night, perhaps this line should be taken instead as referring to her.

34. Presumably this refers to auspicious dates on the almanac.

35. *Yoki tsuma to omoe.* There is a play on words here between "a good wife" and "a good chance."

36. The Assistant Minister presumably goes to Fushimi, where he waits for the rest of his party.

37. *Chūjō no honō no kuruma* ("the Middle Captain's carriage of flames/passion"). The phrase suggests the Lotus Sutra, with its famous portrait of the house of passions, and perhaps the Noh *Kayoi Komachi*, attributed to Kan'ami (1333–84). In that play, a woman rejects her suitor, much as Asukai will refuse the man who actually sends her the carriage.

The boat was a big one.[38] Feeling more dead than alive, Asukai lay weeping in the cabin, wondering whether her lover would visit her parents' home that night. Meanwhile the Assistant Minister arrived. "Come look at this fan," he told the attendants. "This morning, when I went to say goodbye to his lordship the Captain, he told me that he was bringing someone special home tonight. 'Who's going to handle things if you go?' he said.[39] Then he gave this to me, with the poems that he wrote with her in honor of that bright moon on the fifteenth of the Eighth Month. He said that he shouldn't part with it, then gave it to me as a farewell gift." With that, he showed them the fan.

"How strange," Asukai marveled, listening. "I wrote a poem like that on a fan that night, too. I guess I wasn't the only one." When the attendants started passing the fan around, she stole a glimpse at it, only to realize that the poems were the very same ones that she and her lover had written. But that meant that he was the Sagoromo Middle Captain! All those nights that he had come to see her, and she had had no idea. Horrified, Asukai resolved to take the tonsure as soon as the wetnurse left her alone.[40] If the Captain learned the truth, he would never understand and, worse, he would think her beneath contempt. If only she could jump overboard! But no opportunity for this came, and so she simply continued to weep.

That night, Sagoromo took his carriage to her house as usual. Leaving his men with the vehicle, he went to her room, only to find that she was not there. Heart pounding, he asked Mikawa what had happened.[41] "She was very upset," the attendant explained, "and then she disappeared right after you left this morning. Her parents are frantic." The woman handed him a scroll. "She said to give you this letter if you came." As he unrolled it, he saw that the contents were extraordinarily moving, and his eyes strayed to the two poems at the end:

---

38. *Tonobara no onfune.* The crucial word, *tonobara*, has two different meanings. On the one hand, it may indicate a number of nobles (i.e., a larger traveling party), who would in this case be sharing the boat. More likely, given the contrast between this boat and that belonging to Asukai's brother, whom we meet shortly, the Assistant Minister is trading on Sagoromo's connections.

39. *Wadono narade wa, hajihajishiki motenashi o tare ka subeki.* Sagoromo makes no such remark in the text of the story. Perhaps the Assistant Minister is embellishing in order to impress the attendants (and, ultimately, Asukai). Either way, the comment resonates ironically, since his attentions drive Asukai to attempt suicide.

40. *Ama sae menoto no fuzai ni naritaran.* Again, the reference to the wetnurse evokes the Heian subplot.

41. Presumably one of Asukai's attendants. *Mikawa* was the name of a province located in the eastern portion of the current Aichi prefecture. The attendant probably has a relative there or has spent time there herself.

ちぎりあらば又もこん世にめぐりあはんけふはふちせに身をばいるとも

If our vows are real	chigiri araba
once again in the next world	mata mo kon'yo ni
we shall surely meet,	meguriawan
even if today I give	kyō wa fuchise ni
my body to the water's course.[42]	mi o ba iru to mo

はかなくもけふはふちせにいりぬともなからんあとをたれかとはまし

Fragile though I am	hakanaku mo
if today I give myself	kyō wa fuchise ni
to the water's course,	irinu to mo
would that somebody might seek	nakaran ato o
traces of me when I'm gone.	tare ka towamashi

As he read these poems, Sagoromo realized that he might never see her again, and if she did become so much flotsam, what about him, left behind? What should he do? His heart burned within him, his feelings pitiful. Sending the rest of the escort home, he turned to Kanetaka, a member of his personal staff.[43] "Stay with me," he said. "Normally I would rely on the Assistant Minister, but he's left for Tsukushi, and now you're the only one I can trust to stand by me. They're saying that a woman I cared about got upset with me and disappeared, and I want to look for her."

"I'll follow you anywhere," said Kanetaka. How miserable they must have felt as they set out on this unfamiliar path! They visited every last mountain and temple, but it was all for nothing: in five years of searching, they never even heard her name. Sagoromo had known from the beginning that nothing lasts forever, but still he had looked for her.[44] Now he resolved to leave everything behind, cut his hair, and pray for them both in the next life.

---

42. "If this is true love, we'll be reborn together, even if I drown myself." The poem also implies a pun on "this world" (kon'yo) and "the world of the child" (ko no yo), foreshadowing the importance of family ties in this work. This poem and the next do not appear in the three versions of Senji's tale indexed here.

43. Miuchi no mono. In the tale, this character (called Michisue) is the brother of the Assistant Minister.

44. The first half of the line (kono yo no kien wa) is ambiguous. I have taken kien as a speculative form of the verb kiyu (to disappear), but it may name the Buddhist term for a pretext that moves one to take Buddhist vows. In this case, the narrator is saying that Sagoromo knew from the beginning of his search that his loss was a call to prayer, but he looked for Asukai anyway. The line may also foreshadow his discovery of their child, through the pun (ko no yo) noted earlier.

The intervening years had also disappointed Asukai.[45] That night on the boat, she had decided to drown herself in Takasago Bay, but there were too many people around and the chance passed her by. Her next opportunity came at Murotsumi Harbor in Suō where, separating her floor-length hair into five thick strands, she offered one to the clan god, one to the buddhas of the three existences, and said a prayer over the last that she and her lover would be reborn on the same lotus in the next life, no matter how weak their vows had been in this one.[46]

She was just chanting the *nenbutsu* ten times, when a small boat passed by.[47] Although she was a little hesitant, not knowing its passengers, she impulsively decided to try jumping from there, since there was no good spot from which to do so on the big boat.[48] Saying that she had a message for the strangers, she changed ships.[49]

This caused a big commotion on the smaller vessel, since Asukai was so beautiful that they feared she was a transformed being from the palace of the Dragon King.[50] The boat belonged to the son of the Governor-General Middle Counselor who lived on West Tōin near Nijō, a priest who had gone to Tsukushi as the abbot of Anraku Temple years earlier.[51] Now this boat was taking him back to the capital to visit his parents. In short, he was Asukai's older brother. Perhaps the Earth God had taken pity on her,[52] since it was amazing that she now found herself on this boat!

Seeing how distraught she was, the priest asked what was wrong,[53] and she told him the whole story, just as it had happened. As he listened, he realized that she was his sister and was astounded. The gods must have brought her to him! Overjoyed, he told her not to worry, that he would find Sagoromo for her, and he took her back to the capital with him.

---

45. I have added this sentence to make the transition here smoother. The text only has *saru hodo ni saru hodo ni* ("meanwhile, meanwhile" or "as this was happening").

46. These offerings only account for three of the five strands of hair, unless she has symbolically offered one to each of the buddhas of the three existences: past, present, and future.

47. The *nenbutsu*, "Hail, Amida Buddha," appeals to the guardian of the Pure Land, a Buddhist paradise located in the west. This is presumably the final preparation for her leap into the water.

48. Perhaps it has an inconvenient railing. Alternatively, she may have spent too much time in prayer and now there's no good opportunity where she is (i.e., her attendants have returned).

49. The narrator does not explain how she does this. The details are presumably less exciting than those versions of the story in which Asukai accidentally lands in the boat while leaping from the larger vessel.

50. They mistake her for the Dragon King's famously beautiful daughter.

51. The temple was built to house the remains of Sugawara Michizane (845–903), famously exiled to Tsukushi.

52. *Kenrō jishin.*

53. *On'bō.* The narrator refers to him throughout by this generic title, rather than as the abbot.

When they arrived, the priest found an inn for Asukai and went to see their parents, who were delighted to see him. As they reminisced about the years that had passed since he had left, his mother tearfully informed him of his sister's marriage.[54] "She just left for Tsukushi with the Assistant Governor-General, the son of the Sagoromo Middle Captain's wetnurse. We'd been together ever since she was born, and now that she's gone, I miss her so much! If you hadn't come to visit, I don't know what I would have done."

The priest saw his chance. "Amazingly enough," he remarked, "when I was passing through Murotsumi in Suō, she came onto my boat, trying to drown herself. I brought her back with me, since she's obviously still very childish, and left her at an inn. You can come get her quietly tonight."

His parents were furious. "What? You must be lying. You probably just got up to some mischief and stole someone's daughter, and you don't even have the nerve to say so in the first place!" They glared at him, irate. The priest had been hoping to hide Asukai with them, but his parents refused to discuss the matter further. "Get out!" they shouted. "You're no son of ours. Consider yourself an orphan from now on!" They chased him out of the house as if they meant it. The priest had no choice but to leave, heartsick.

When he got back to the inn, he told Asukai what had happened. "I deserve this," she said. "But I feel terrible that now our parents are angry at you, too."

"Things never work out in this world as we want them to," he consoled her. "I've wished I could see you for thirteen years, so to have come all this way without getting to talk to you would have been the real disappointment. From now on, you are my only family, and you must rely on me in the same way. I'm going to go find the Middle Captain." Leaving the gifts that he had brought from Tsukushi for his parents, his own valuables, and his sister with the landlord, he put on traveling clothes and set out after Sagoromo. Asukai wanted to die on the spot, but since this was out of her hands, she stayed where she was and, in time, safely gave birth to a splendid son. The boy's face was the copy of his father's, and for five years he was her only comfort as she waited day and night for her brother to come back.

The priest looked everywhere, from mountain hermitages to seaside huts, but nowhere did he so much as hear Sagoromo's name mentioned. At last, he reluctantly returned to the capital, where Asukai and the wetnurse were still caring for the child. "I did my best," he said. "For five years I've barely stopped to rest, constantly soaked with rain and dew while I looked

---

54. They refer to her as *midai*, short for *midaidokoro*, the wife of a man of high rank.

for him, and I haven't so much as heard someone mention his name. It's time to give up."

While the priest had been gone, hope had given Asukai the strength to keep on living, but now the years of worry caught up with her and she grew weak. Alienated from her parents and not knowing where her lover had gone, she felt adrift and gave herself up to tears.

Uncertain whether to pray for her happiness in this life or the next, the priest set out to pray before the Great Buddha.[55] On his seventh night there, he chanted the Lotus Sutra until dawn in a wonderful voice, then loudly stated his petition: "Hail, all you great gods of Japan! As a reward for my seven days of pilgrimage, may my sister's wish be granted. If her lover is still alive, may she meet him one more time. If he is dead, may my efforts serve as a catalyst to set him on the path toward enlightenment." As the priest was rubbing his rosary beads, Sagoromo arrived in Nara, resolved to atone for his five years of sinful longing by taking the tonsure. He had just begun to pray before the Great Buddha when he heard the priest's impressive chanting of the sutras and noticed that the voice seemed somehow familiar.

"Where are you from," he asked warmly, "and why are you praying so intently?"

The priest had no idea that this was Sagoromo and so answered briefly. "My parents disowned me, and since I had nowhere else to turn in this cruel world, I came here."

"But how could someone so admirable anger his parents?" Sagoromo pressed.

"I tried to help someone close to me, and this is where it led."

Sagoromo tried again. "What is your name?"

"I guess it doesn't hurt to tell you," the priest replied. "My father is the Governor-General Middle Counselor who lives on West Tōin near Nijō. My sister and I are all alone now and . . ." But before he could finish, they heard an old nun from behind the main hall, calling urgently for the priest, and he started off, looking worried.

"Where are you going?" called Sagoromo.

"I'll be right back," the priest assured him.

The Middle Captain was delighted. "Now I can finally get some answers," he thought, his heart pounding in his chest. But the priest did not return. Disappointed, Sagoromo went to find the nun who had called him away. "Does anyone know where that priest went?" he asked. It was

---

55. That is, the Daibutsu, located in Nara.

moving to see how dejected he was when he realized that the man had vanished. When Sagoromo finally found the nun, he was as happy as if he had met Jizō in hell.[56] Grabbing hold of the woman's sleeve, he asked, "Who was the priest you called away just now, and where did he go? What did you say to him?"

"I just live here," she said. "A traveler asked me to get the priest chanting the sutras, so I did."

"But what did he say?" Sagoromo insisted.

"Well, I did overhear that the priest's sister was dying, and that this might be his last chance to see her. He was horrified and said that he had been on retreat here to pray for her recovery, then he hurried off in tears. I felt bad for him and asked him where he was from, as he was leaving, and he said 'Tokiwa.'"

When Sagoromo heard this, he immediately set out for Tokiwa where, at the top of a mountain, he found a lonely hut that looked as if people of taste might live there. As he looked further, he noticed a small stone monument in front of the hermitage, a memorial that clearly had not been there long. Sagoromo wondered who had died. How sad the deceased's parents and other loved ones must be, he thought. It was only life that changed; grief was always present. As he continued to gaze at the grave marker, he heard what sounded like someone tearfully chanting the Lotus Sutra inside the hermitage and, straining his ears, he recognized the voice of the priest he had met and lost at Nara. Filled with hope, he knocked on the door.

"Who is it?" came the reply.

"A traveler," Sagoromo replied. "Please give me shelter for the night." The priest came out, startled to see his guest.

"What a strange bond we must have!" he exclaimed. "Didn't I see you at Nara?"

"It is indeed a very strange bond," Sagoromo returned. "I was so curious to hear the rest of your story that I followed you when you disappeared, and the gods led me here." His delight was obvious. "And what do you call this place?"

"Tokiwa," the priest answered. "My sister was living here, but for the last four or five years she's done nothing but grieve from dawn to dusk, and she finally wasted away. Today is the seventh day since her death. The grave marker over there is hers." As he said this, he hid his face in his sleeves and wept.

---

56. The bodhisattva Jizō (Ksitigarbha) was said to rescue souls in torment.

So the deceased person was Asukai, the woman he had longed for all this time. Sagoromo broke down and told the priest the whole story.

"You're Sagoromo?" The priest was astonished. "How terrible! When I think of how she suffered!" They wrung out their sleeves together as they wept.

Sagoromo finally spoke. "Did she have a child?"

"She did," the priest confirmed. "It was a boy, and since they say that children shouldn't go into mourning until they're seven, and both of his parents were of noble birth, I sent him to live with Her Highness."[57]

"I'd like to at least get a look at him."

"The boy isn't like other children," the priest cautioned. "He was really upset when his mother died, and I understand that he's always going into the garden and breaking off flowers to offer to the Buddha for her. He chants the *nenbutsu*, too."

Sagoromo went to the woman's estate, following the priest's advice to steal a glimpse when he could, since the boy was always in the flower garden. Thinking that the sight would be a good way to remember the boy's mother, he even paid a formal call on the child's guardian, Princess Hansei, who sent someone out to talk with him.[58] "Where have you come from?"[59] asked the attendant.

"I'm from the capital," he replied. "Since I happened to be passing by, I thought I would pay the Princess a visit." They set out a mat for him near the middle gate and offered him some refreshment.[60] Although he had not yet told them who he was, since he was from the capital, they treated him kindly; in fact, since his good looks suggested his high rank, they entertained him in style.

As Sagoromo looked out at the western half of the grounds, he saw two children playing there, one about seven and the other close to five. The five-year-old, a boy, had run into the near garden, by a small chicken missing some of its feathers and skin.[61]

---

57. Technically, the priest only says that he sent the child to live in the home of a high-ranking person (*gosho*). We later learn that this is a princess, although the narrator never clearly identifies her.

58. *Hansei no miya.* The narrator does not give any other information.

59. This is probably a polite way of asking his name and his business.

60. This location is convenient, since it allows Sagoromo to see into the garden and thus spot his son.

61. Because of its size, this bird is probably at the bottom of the literal pecking order and shows the signs of it. The reference suggests some familiarity with actual barnyard behavior, in both the writer and the readers that s/he expects to appreciate it.

みなしごとはねなきとりとくらぶればなをみなしごぞかなしかりける

An orphaned child and	*minashigo to*
a chicken missing its feathers	*hane naki tori to*
when I compare them,	*kurabureba*
it is still the orphaned child	*nao minashigo zo*
who is the sadder of the two.[62]	*kanashikarikeru*

After reciting this verse, the child started weeping and went inside.

"That must be him." The Middle Captain called the boy over, who came to him without the slightest sign of fear and sat on his lap. Sagoromo looked intently at him and asked where his parents were. The boy said nothing, but his tears rained down. "What's the matter?" Sagoromo asked.

"They told me that my father died when I was still in my mother's womb. Then she died pining for him seven days ago. I wish you were my father." He gazed affectionately into Sagoromo's face.

Although they had been separated since birth, the call of blood must have been strong, for Sagoromo seemed drawn to the boy as well and held him tightly. "I am your father. I am the man your mother was pining for."

"You are?!" The tone was affectionate.

Sagoromo wrung out his priestly sleeves.[63] "Did your mother have any last words?"

"Just before she died, she took me on her lap and said how sad she was to leave me behind when I was already defenseless without a father. 'I hate to make you an orphan,' she said, 'but even after I die, remember, if your father is still alive, you may be reunited. Grow up strong and pray for my rebirth in paradise.' Then she said that people who die heartbroken never attain enlightenment, and told me to tell you, if we ever met, that it was your fault that my mother died. She left something for me to show you, too. You're supposed to copy the 'Greater Vehicle' on it five times.[64] It's what they call a lover's complaint."[65]

---

62. "I have it worse than even this poor chicken, because I have no parents." Court tales sometimes use the phrase *hane no shita* ("beneath the wings") as a metaphor for parental care. The boy's poem thus suggests his (supposed) orphaned state. This poem is almost certainly unique to the medieval cycle; moreover, it only appears in some lineages.

63. *Jōe no sode.* The phrase is ambiguous. It may refer to any ceremonially pure robes worn during festivals or religious services, or (written with different characters) it may name the outermost robe worn by a priest. Since Sagoromo is presumably still wearing the robes that he wore to Nara where he planned to take the tonsure, they are probably the latter.

64. *Gobu no daijōkyō.* Alternatively, a five-part version of this sutra. While there are roughly six hundred Mahayana or "Greater Vehicle" sutras extant, the phrase commonly refers to the Lotus Sutra. This would make sense here, since the Lotus (evoked earlier in the story with the reference to the Dragon King's daughter) famously suggests that women can attain enlightenment.

65. *Koizukushi.* An exhaustive treatment of the subject of love, here probably filled with lover's complaints.

"Well, let's see it." The boy went in and returned with ten scrolls. As Sagoromo read them, his eyes clouded with tears, and his heart ached, until he could hardly make out what he saw.

"Just imagine what the other two scrolls were like," the boy said, in a grown-up manner that pierced Sagoromo's heart.[66] Meanwhile, the Princess peeked at them from inside, amazed to see Sagoromo and the boy weeping. Since she couldn't hear what they were talking about, she sent someone out to ask, and Sagoromo told her the whole story. "I'd like to have the boy to remember his mother by," he said. "Once I've raised him, I can send him back into your service. I don't know how to repay you for looking after him until now."

"Then you're the Sagoromo Middle Captain," the Princess replied, wringing out her sleeves. "I've never heard such a sad story."

Sagoromo and his son returned to the priest's hermitage. "He's so grown-up, and understands so much, that I couldn't bear to part with him," the hero explained to the priest. If I had abandoned this child, who meant so much to his mother, when would I have ever been able to find him again?"[67] His tears rained down again as he spoke. How wonderful to have found his son! And how terrible not to be able to see Asukai herself! He felt powerless, and even though he knew it was a very strange request, he asked the priest to dig up her corpse and show it to him.

At first the priest refused. "Even without us doing something like that, people who die of passion must endlessly repeat the cycle of rebirth without gaining enlightenment. How can you talk of unearthing her corpse?! It's terribly sinful, and we mustn't do it."

Sagoromo turned to his son. "Find a way to make the priest dig her up and show her to me one more time. If you don't, I will abandon you and go off somewhere, and you don't want to lose your father after only just meeting him, do you?"

The boy threw himself on the priest in tears and, unable to refuse, the priest started digging. Before long, he brought up the coffin. "She's been dead for seven days now," he thought to himself. "She must be a gruesome sight. What a pity it would be for the Captain to see that and be revolted by her." Doing reverence in the four directions, he began to pray. "All hail the Earth God! May the merit I have attained through my years of practice let Sagoromo see Asukai as she was before, even if she is dead." He gave it his

---

66. I am not sure about this passage. Sagoromo seems to ask about two missing scrolls, just as he does in the tale. However, neither the boy nor the narrator says more about this. I have assigned lines based on the level of honorifics and tried to fit the context.

67. At this point the line blurs into the narrator's speech, with the character apparently referring to himself with both an honorific phrase (*mikokoro no uchi*) and a humble verb (*kanashiku koso sōroe*). I have reassigned this line to the narrator.

best. Then, sending Sagoromo and the boy a little way away, he raised the lid of the coffin to find that Asukai had not changed a bit. She looked perfectly healthy, as if she had simply fallen asleep; even her face, which had so worried him, was beautiful, so he called the others over to look at her, too.

Sagoromo and his son spoke to her as if she were alive. "For the last four or five years, I've been wandering everywhere because of you," wept the hero, taking her on his lap. "Now do you understand how much I love you? I've come all this way to see you. Why won't you wake up?"

The boy took hold of his mother's hand in tears. "Wake up!" he pleaded. "Dad's finally here." Needless to say, it was an extremely moving sight, and watching him, Sagoromo felt even worse. He resumed badgering the priest.

"I've heard that, with the merit attained by religious practice, one can drive out even strange spirits and bring the dead back to life. Why aren't you praying for that?"

"I understand what you want," the priest answered, "and if she had only died recently, I would pray just as you wish, even if I thought it was hopeless. But she died seven days ago, after wearing herself out with longing for you for four or five years. Prayer is not going to help."

"But people usually look different even right after they die," Sagoromo persisted. "How can someone who's been dead seven days look as beautiful as she does? I'm sure that the gods and buddhas are behind it. Please, just try praying." So the priest paid reverence in the four directions and began to pray.

"Ever since I left my mother's womb," he intoned, "I have upheld the precepts. I have stayed pure and never slackened in my practice. May this woman come back to life before the Captain's eyes, even if her karma is fixed.[68] May he see this sign even if she dies immediately afterwards. Hail to you, gods and spirits of Japan, take pity on us." As he spoke, her breast grew slightly warm to the touch. Amazed and delighted, Sagoromo ordered the priest to pray harder, and he chanted for all he was worth. Perhaps the Earth God was listening, too, because even though Asukai's karma was fixed, she came back to life.

Tears come first in joy and in sorrow, and here there was no holding them back. Asukai looked all around her, feeling as if she were dreaming, and saw her son and the priest. And there was Sagoromo by her pillow! Since she had often seen him there in her dreams, she did not realize at first that she was

68. *Jōgō.* Inevitable karma/karmic consequences. There are apparently two ways of defining this, depending on whether one focuses on its causes or its time of fulfillment (in this or some future life). According to *Soka Gakkai Dictionary of Buddhism,* causes include "actions motivated by exceptionally strong earthly desires" and "actions causing harm to ones parents." The priest knows that Asukai is guilty of these counts.

awake, but she gradually came to her senses, marveling at the strangeness of it all. Since they couldn't leave things as they were, the others took her inside and fussed over her until she felt more like herself.[69] Even strangers would have wet their sleeves with tears listening to them talk about the past. Then Asukai started to glare at Sagoromo with obvious resentment, although she was deeply sinful herself.[70]

"I threw my life away and caused my parents endless grief for you," he defended himself. "And it's my love that brought us back together just now." She had to admit that he was right, so they placed their son between them and resumed talking of their old lives and of what they would do next, crying all the while.

After two or three days, they realized that they couldn't go on like this, so they sent Kanetaka to Sagoromo's home to request an escort. As it happened, the Minister was just then chanting the *nenbutsu* and some sutras for his son's benefit. When he saw Kanetaka, he was stunned. "Kanetaka?" Before the word was out of his mouth, the Minister had grabbed the man's sleeve. "Where is the Middle Captain?" he demanded, in tears. "It's cruel that children don't care for their parents the way that we care for them, especially when it's so terribly sinful for us to drag out our lives worrying like this!" Kanetaka told him the whole story, and the Minister, overjoyed, called for a carriage—but he was too eager to see his son to wait for it.

Instead, he ordered Kanetaka to accompany him and ran off to Tokiwa himself, in bare feet. When he reached the place where Sagoromo was, he launched into a litany of complaints. "Who do you think I am, abandoning me for all these years? And still I'm happy to have dragged out my useless life long enough to see you again like this!" Sagoromo was deeply ashamed, admitting that only a parent would have come all that way barefoot. Eventually the carriage arrived with Sagoromo's mother.

"They say that a child is a treasure," she wept, "but when you've suffered as I have. . . . Even so, even if he is your enemy, it's still a wonderful thing to have a child." It was moving to see her sweep the little boy into her arms so affectionately, and although the escort had brought several carriages, Asukai, Sagoromo, their son, and Sagoromo's parents all squeezed into one vehicle to return to the Minister's residence.[71] Everyone who saw them, high-ranking or humble, kind and cruel, was deeply moved.

---

69. *Shiki no hito.* Literally, (more like) a real person.
70. As noted earlier, she died in the grip of attachment, a particularly sinful death.
71. Alternatively, they may go straight to the palace. The word used here, *gosho*, is ambiguous.

When the Emperor heard about all of this, he was astonished. "You only hear such moving stories if you live in the world," he reflected, and then, relinquishing his title to Sagoromo's son, he became a monk and retired to Mount Ogura.[72] The new emperor promoted his father from captain to minister and made his uncle the priest the abbot of Enryakuji, awarding the provinces of Iyo and Harima to Princess Sei.[73] The splendor of the entire company was almost frightening, and in fact, right afterward, Asukai—who had seen the horrors of hell—cut off her long hair and became a nun.[74] Sagoromo, who had wanted to take vows for some time, did so with her. Not wishing to be shown up by younger persons, his parents followed suit.

After taking the tonsure, they all went to live on Mount Ogura with the retired emperor, where they drew water from the valleys and picked flowers on the peaks. Three years passed as they practiced their devotions together and then, one fall, twenty-five bodhisattvas led by Seishi and Kannon came to usher them to the Pure Land.[75] It was an extraordinary sight.[76]

While it has long been said that women cannot become buddhas, Asukai was revealed as an avatar of Dainichi,[77] while Sagoromo became Nichigatsu and his father and mother appeared as avatars of Fudō and the Wish-Fulfilling Kannon, respectively.[78] Thanks to their light, Princess Hansei became an

---

72. This mountain is strongly associated with Teika, who compiled a famous set of poems there. It also appears in the play translated in chapter 4, probably written at the same time as some of the earlier narratives in this cycle.

73. *Sei no miya* is presumably a mistake for Hansei, the name used earlier. These are lucrative assignments.

74. Women's hair was traditionally seen as a symbol of their sinful sexuality and worldly attachments.

75. Seishi (in Sanskrit, Mahāsthāmaprāpta) and Kannon (Avalokiteśvara) are the bodhisattvas of wisdom and compassion, respectively. Typically, they descend with Amida Buddha and the other bodhisattvas to welcome the believer to Amida's Pure Land. However, the text makes no mention of Amida, perhaps to highlight the Buddhist deities discussed next.

76. This outcome is strongly reminiscent of sections of *Tales of the Heike* (*Heike monogatari*, ca. 1371), both in the depiction of fellow practitioners attaining enlightenment simultaneously and in the focus on a female figure. Perhaps this association explains Asukai's appearance in a "Mount Ōhara carriage" at the start of the text; Ōhara is the setting of *Heike*'s final chapter, which depicts several such events. Those women, however, are not shown to be manifestations of Buddhist deities; this is a typically late medieval twist.

77. Mahavairocana, literally, the Great Sun, and the source of all other buddhas and bodhisattvas, sometimes identified with Amaterasu. An avatar (*keshin*, literally, transformed body) is a manifestation of a buddha in the form most helpful to those whom that buddha hopes to save.

78. There are two options for Sagoromo's new identity: Nichigatsu jōmyōtoku butsu (Sun Moon Pure Bright Virtue) and Nichigatsu tōmyō butsu (Sun Moon Bright). The second figure, described in the introduction to the Lotus Sutra, is perhaps the one meant here. Interestingly, Sagoromo is simply said to become this deity, not to become its avatar as with all of the other characters. Nyoirin Kannon, one of the bodhisattva's many forms, is said to save with her eponymous jewel and wheel. Fudō (in Sanskrit, Acala), a fierce guardian deity, is said to be immovable in his virtue.

avatar of Bishamon,[79] and as for the boy, he turned out to have been their own little Sacred Kannon, appearing in order to save all sentient beings.[80] He led all living things to the path of enlightenment.

How could anything this wonderful ever happen without children? Since the righteous end up helping even the very sinful to succeed in this life and to become buddhas in the next, *The Sagoromo Middle Captain* is a splendid book. It is also deeply moving and elegant. When men and women love each other deeply and show compassion until the end, how can they be judged inferior to anyone, whatever their social status? For more details, see the conclusion to the book.[81]

Copied on a lucky day of the Third Month of Keichō 2 [1597].

---

79. Bishamonten, one of the four heavenly kings that also serve as protective deities in Buddhism and, in Japan, one of the seven gods of fortune. Since he is associated in both roles with warriors and warfare, Princess Hansei's connection to him seems to be her wealth.

80. Sagoromo's son apparently took holy orders with his family, although the narrator didn't specify this earlier. The boy's new identity puns on Shōkannon, which denotes Sacred Kannon, one of the bodhisattva's manifestations, but also puns on "small Kannon," a nod to his youth.

81. *Oku no gekkan.* Literally, the second volume within the book. Since this text is in one quire, I'm not sure what to make of this, other than as a gesture to the kinds of hidden secrets discussed in the commentary presented in chapter 5.

CHAPTER 2

Sagoromo

The Wisconsin Collection

Overview

As detailed in my introduction, this new collection translates the forty-one overlapping poems from *The Tale of Sagoromo* featured in *The Genji-Sagoromo Contest* (ca. 1206), compiled by Fujiwara Teika, and the extant volumes of *Collection of Wind-Blown Leaves* (ca. 1271), often ascribed to his son Tameie but requested and enthusiastically supported by Empress Kitsu-shi and her staff. I also translate the verses' competing headnotes, supplied by the compilers. My title names my institution, to avoid the confusion that a more traditional label, like "New Contest in Forty-one Rounds," might generate.

I group the poems and headnotes by the tale's books, although *Contest* simply matches these verses to others in *Genji*, and *Collection*, as seen below, assigns them to categories: in addition to longing (the dominant theme in both compilations), religion and the seasons, particularly winter and summer—not considered as poetic as spring and fall, with which Senji framed *The Tale of Sagoromo* itself. The majority of the material comes from books 1 and 2, which supply thirteen poems each. Book 3 fares almost as well, providing ten verses. Book 4 only yields five shared poems, although the separate totals in my sources are higher. Japanese versions of poems come from Teika's *Contest* unless the verse in *Collection* is very different; in that case, I reproduce both. I typically do not note differences in alternate versions of a given headnote. Note that *Collection* typically refers to Sagoromo by his last post, emperor. *Contest* prefers his iconic office of middle captain. Both choices are typical for their respective works. Also typical are *Collection*'s longer headnotes.[1]

My base texts appear in *OMS*. This edition is cross-referenced and lightly annotated. The text of *Contest* reflects one in Teika's hand held by Hokuni Bunko. The text of *Collection* reflects the eighteen-volume version held by the Imperial Household Agency's Shoryōbu archive. I have also consulted the version of *Contest* found at the end of *SNKZ*, vol. 1, based on the text held by Shigure-tei Bunko, and the version of *Collection* in *KKT*. It uses the twenty-volume Tankaku-bon. Like the use of poetic categories, this number of books recalls imperial collections of poetry, making *Collection* (effectively) an imperial anthology of tale-verse. Italicized material in the headnotes reflects my annotations, informed by the editors of my base or reference texts.

Translation

Poems from Book 1 of *The Tale of Sagoromo*

POEM 1: SAGOROMO

Contest, Round 16 | At the rooms of the Genji Princess, while looking at the kerria roses:

Collection, #1065 (Love) | Breaking off a spray of kerria rose, with the intention of showing it to the Kamo Priestess, and saying that even though these vows are unspoken they must have begun to bloom:

いかにせむ言はぬ色なる花なれば心のうちを知る人もなし

What then should I do?	*ika ni semu*
Since this flower has a hue	*iwanu iro naru*
which we do not name,	*hana nareba*
there is nobody who knows	*kokoro no uchi o*
the feelings in my heart.[2]	*shiru hito mo nashi*

1. See Oguri, "*Monogatari hyakuban utaawase* no kotobagaki to *Fūyō wakashū* no kotobagaki."

2. *OMS Collection*, *KKT*, and *SNKS* (1:10) end *shiru hito zo naki*. *SNKZ* (1:18) ends *shiru hito wa nashi*. *NKBT* (30) is as above. This poem is noted in the commentary in chapter 5; see gloss 12.

POEM 2: SAISHŌ FROM THE HOUSEHOLD OF THE PRINCELY MINISTER OF CENTRAL AFFAIRS

Contest, Round 10 | When he was a middle captain of the second rank, and his carriage was passing by, taking an iris down from her eaves:

    Collection, #160 (Summer) | When the Emperor was still a commoner, on the evening of the fourth day of the Fifth Month, on the road home from the palace, taking an iris from her eaves and sending it to him from the gallery:

しらぬまのあやめはそれと見えずともよもぎがかどは過ぎずもあらなむ

At Shiranuma	*Shiranuma no*
when irises cannot be seen	*ayame wa sore to*
for what they are,	*miezu to mo*
would you ever not pass by	*yomogi ga kado wa*
the gate covered in mugwort?[3]	*sugizu mo aranamu*

POEM 3: SAGOROMO

Contest, Round 20 | When he was a middle captain of the second rank, to the Ippon Princess:

    Collection, #1074 (Love) | On the fifth day of the Fifth Month, sent to a woman:

思ひつつ岩垣沼のあやめ草みごもりながら朽ちや果てなむ

While thinking of you,	*omoitsutsu*
like the iris-grasses of	*Iwagakinuma no*
Iwagaki Marsh,	*ayamegusa*
I wonder if, still water-logged,	*migomorinagara*
I will finally rot away.[4]	*kuchi ya hatenamu*

---

3. *OMS Collection* attributes the poem to Kozaishō and has the particle *o*, not *wa*, in line 4. *KKT* and *SNKS* (1:22) have *moto*, not *kado*, in the same line, with *wa*. *SNKZ* (1:32) and *NKBT* (39) are as above. This poem is noted in chapter 5; see gloss 54. The speaker, an attendant, dares the hero to stop at her employer's nondescript house. There is also a pun on Shiranuma, a place name that suggests "while not knowing" (*shiranu ma*).

4. *SNKZ Contest* has *omoedomo* in line 1. *OMS Collection, KKT, SNKS* (1:24), and *SNKZ* (1:35) have *kuchihatene to ya* in line 5. *NKBT* (40) is as above. This poem is noted in the commentary in chapter 5; see gloss 65. This is the same woman whom Sagoromo later unwillingly marries.

POEM 4: SAGOROMO

Contest, Round 55 | After a night when he was entirely unable to sleep, upon hearing a nightingale:
   Collection, #152 (Summer) | In the dawn sky, faintly hearing the call of a nightingale:

夜もすがら嘆き明かしてほととぎす鳴く音をだにも聞く人もがな

All throughout the night	*yomosugara*
grieving, then greeting dawn so—	*nageki akashite*
poor nightingale!	*hototogisu*
Would that there were someone who	*naku ne o dani mo*
might listen to your cries, at least.	*kiku hito mogana*

   The version in *Collection of Wind-Blown Leaves* is considerably different:

夜もすがら物や思へるほととぎす天の岩戸をあけがたに鳴く

All throughout the night	*yomosugara*
are you worrying about love,	*mono ya omoeru*
poor nightingale?	*hototogisu*
You cry with the opening of	*ama no iwato o*
the dawn and heaven's rocky door.[5]	*akegata ni naku*

POEM 5: SAGOROMO

Contest, Round 42 | When the Kamo Priestess was still called the Genji Princess:
   Collection, #806 (Love) | To a woman with whom he had secretly shared his thoughts:

我ばかり思ひこがれて年経やと室の八島の煙にも問へ

Will the years pass by	*ware bakari*
smoldering with love for you	*omoikogarete*
as in my present state?	*toshi fu ya to*
Ask the smoke that rises from	*Muro no yashima no*
the Eight Islands at Muro.[6]	*keburi ni mo toe*

---

   5. *KKT* and *SNKS* (1:42) are as in *OMS Contest*. *SNKZ* (1:55) and *NKBT* (53) are closer to *OMS Collection* excepting line 2: they have *mono ya omou to* and *mono o ya omou*, respectively.

   6. The tributes agree. The three versions of the tale vary in line 1. *SNKS* (1:45) and *SNKZ* (1:60) have *kaku bakari*. *NKBT* (56) has *ika bakari*.

POEM 6: SAGOROMO

Contest, Round 11 | Having drawn his carriage into Asukai's lodgings, where the smoke from the mosquito smudges was stifling:

Collection, #193 (Summer) | Having drawn his carriage into Asukai's lodgings, where even the smoke from the mosquito smudges was difficult to bear:

我が心かねて空にや満ちぬらむ行く方知らぬ宿の蚊遣火

This poor heart of mine—	*waga kokoro*
has it already grown full,	*kanete sora ni ya*
like the smoky sky?	*michinuramu*
I do not know where it will end,	*yuku kata shiranu*
the mosquito smudge at this house.[7]	*yado no kayaribi*

POEM 7: SAGOROMO

Contest, Round 19 | Around summer, while visiting the Genji Princess and hearing the cry of the cicadas in the trees:

Collection, #1084 (Love) | Topic unknown:

声立ててなかぬばかりぞ物思ふ身はうつせみに劣りやはする

Without my voice,	*koe tatete*
without crying at all	*nakanu bakari zo*
I long for you.	*mono omou*
Am I no better than	*mi wa utsusemi ni*
an empty locust's shell?[8]	*otori ya wa suru*

POEM 8: SAGOROMO

Contest, Round 25 | At Asukai's lodgings:

Collection, #863 (Love) | Composed to express [*say*] how difficult it was to spend night after night separated from a woman he was seeing in secret:

---

7. *OMS Collection* has *yukue mo shiranu* in line 4. *KKT*, *SNKS* (1:62–63), and *NKBT* (69) are as above. *SNKZ* (80–81) has *michiniken* in line 3. Sagoromo compares his love for Asukai to the smoke from the fires lit to repel insects.

8. All seven texts agree. See *SNKS* (1:74), *SNKZ* (1:95), and *NKBT* (78).

あひ見ては袖ぬれまさるさ夜衣一夜ばかりも隔てずもがな

After I see you,	*aimite wa*
the sleeves grow wetter still	*sode nuremasaru*
on my sleeping robe	*sayogoromo*
if only we could never part	*hitoyo bakari mo*
even for a single night.[9]	*hedatezu mogana*

POEM 9: ASUKAI

Contest, Round 48 | On the dawn she departed, led away by her wetnurse:

   Collection, #972 (Love) | When the Emperor was still a commoner, at a place that he had been visiting in secret, on the dawn when she was leaving for somewhere else against her will and—just as she wanted to say that the moment had come—heard a rooster cry out:

天の戸をやすらひにこそ出でしかとゆふつけ鳥よ問はば答へよ

The heavenly door—	*ama no to o*
only with hesitation	*yasurai ni koso*
did I leave it behind.	*ideshika to*
Tell him that if he should ask,	*yūtsukedori yo*
rooster wearing mulberry floss.[10]	*towaba kotaeyo*

POEM 10: ASUKAI

Contest, Round 34 | Inside a boat against her wishes and thinking that her life was at its end, she added this to his fan, next to where he had written, "Boatman as you row across / cut the oar-straps loose":

   Collection, #1045 (Love) | Inside a boat against her wishes, and thinking that her life was at its end, she added this to the Emperor's fan, next to where he had written, "Boatman as you row across":

梶を絶え命も絶ゆと知しらせばや涙の海に沈む舟人

With the oar-straps cut,	*kajio tae*
my life is also cut short—	*inochi mo tayu to*
if I could tell him that!	*shirasebaya*
Drowning in a sea of tears,	*namida no umi ni*
a passenger upon this boat.[11]	*shizumu funabito*

---

   9. The tributes agree. *SNKS* (1:95) has *nuresomuru* in line 2. *SNKZ* (1:121) and *NKBT* (95) have *aimineba* in line 1.

   10. *SNKZ* Contest and *SNKZ* (1:132) have *yūtsukedori no* in line 4. *SNKS* (1:105) and *NKBT* (102) are as above.

   11. All seven texts agree. See *SNKS* (1:112), *SNKZ* (1:140), and *NKBT* (107). None of the series mentions the excerpted poem.

Poem 11: Sagoromo

Contest, Round 63 │ After Asukai had disappeared:
  Collection, #1120 (Love) │ Topic unknown:

しきたへの枕ぞ浮きてながれける妹なき床の秋の寝覚に

My bark-cloth pillow	*shikitae no*
floated away on my tears;	*makura zo ukite*
now I lie awake	*nagarekeru*
on my bed without my love	*imo naki toko no*
all throughout the autumn night.[12]	*aki no nezame ni*

Poem 12: Sagoromo

Contest, Round 54 │ After Asukai had vanished:
  Collection, #349 (Autumn) │ Lost in worries and staring off into the distance, he composed this at the time when the treetops, too, change color:

せく袖にもりて涙や染めつらむ梢色増す秋の夕暮

These sleeves that hide grief,	*seku sode ni*
have they sprung a leak and let	*morite namida ya*
tears stain them anew?	*sometsuramu*
Treetops bring out deeper hues	*kozue iro masu*
during the autumn twilight.[13]	*aki no yūgure*

Poem 13: Asukai

Contest, Round 91 │ On the boat:
  Collection, #1046 (Love) │ At the same time [*see poem #10*], added as she resolved to jump into the sea:

早き瀬の底の水屑となりにきと扇の風に吹きも伝へよ

I have now become	*hayaki se no*
weeds at the bottom of	*soko no mikuzu to*
this rapid strait.	*nariniki to*
Carry him these tidings, please,	*ōgi no kaze ni*
on the breeze sent by this fan.[14]	*fuki mo tsutaeyo*

---

12. *OMS Collection* and *SNKZ* (1:146) have *kimi* instead of *imo* in line 4. *KKT* has *nagarenuru* in line 3. *SNKS* (1:117) and *NKBT* (110) feature both alternatives. The former also exchanges *mo* for *zo* in line 2.
    13. All seven texts agree. See *SNKS* (1:119), *SNKZ* (1:148), and *NKBT* (113).
    14. *OMS Collection* and *SNKZ* (1:152) have *ni* instead of *to* in line 3 and *yo* rather than *ni* in line 4. *KKT* has *ni* in both spots, splitting the difference. *SNKS* (1:122) and *NKBT* (115) have *yo* in line 4.

Poems from Book 2 of *The Tale of Sagoromo*

POEM 14: SAGOROMO

Contest, Round 3 | When he was worrying about the Ippon Princess [*this should be Asukai*], who was still secret and whose whereabouts were unclear, he saw the frost grow deeper on the grasses of remembrance beneath the pampas grass:

　　Collection, #385 (Winter) | When he was worrying about a woman whose whereabouts were unclear, and seeing the frost grow deeper on the grass beneath the pampas grass:

尋ぬべき草の原さへ霜枯れて誰に問はまし道芝の露

There where I should search,	*tazunubeki*
even those grassy fields	*kusa no hara sae*
have withered from the frost;	*shimogarete*
whom now will I ask for help,	*tare ni towamashi*
dew atop the roadside grass?[15]	*michishiba no tsuyu*

POEM 15: SAGOROMO

Contest, Round 2 | When he was a major captain, to the Second Princess in her Kokiden apartments:

　　Collection, #850 (Love) | After leaving signs of his visit [*in the rooms of*] the Second Princess of the Saga Retired Emperor:

死にかへり待つに命ぞ絶えぬべきなかなかなにに頼みそめけむ

Returning from death	*shinikaeri*
while I wait, my own life seems	*matsu ni inochi zo*
likely to give out.	*taenubeki*
On what, exactly, then	*naka naka nani ni*
did I begin to depend?[16]	*tanomisomekemu*

POEM 16: SAGOROMO

Contest, Round 38 | To the Second Princess:

　　Collection, #913 (Love) | On the morning after he secretly approached the Second Princess:

The commentary in chapter 5 mentions a poem by the Sen'yōden Consort (whom Sagoromo appears to have seduced before the tale opens) with strikingly similar imagery; see gloss 69 (*uki ni nomi*).

15. All seven texts agree on the text of the poem. See *SNKS* (1:127), *SNKZ* (1:157), and *NKBT* (119). The *OMS* editor marks the mistake in the poem's headnote, which may have been inspired by confusion between Asukai and her daughter, who later inherits the Ippon Princess's title.

16. The tributes agree. *SNKS* (1:140) has *tanome* in line 5. *SNKZ* (1:173) and *NKBT* (129) are as above.

うたた寝をなかなか夢と思はばや覚めて合はする人もありやと

Dropping off to sleep—	*utatane o*
if only I could see this, too,	*naka naka yume to*
as a kind of dream!	*omowabaya*
Then I could have it read	*samete awasuru*
and perhaps meet her in life.[17]	*hito mo ari ya to*

POEM 17: SAGOROMO

Contest, Round 64 | After Asukai disappeared:

 Collection, #1025 (Love) | Unable to forget Asukai, and wishing that he could seek her out, even among the weeds at the bottom of the sea:

思ひやる心いづくに逢ひぬらむ海山とだに知らぬ別れに

Sending out my thoughts,	*omoiyaru*
I wonder where my heart has gone	*kokoro izuku ni*
and where we two will meet—	*ainuramu*
not even knowing if	*umiyama to dani*
sea or mountains separate us.[18]	*shiranu wakare ni*

POEM 18: THE SECOND PRINCESS

Contest, Round 89 | When she was not feeling like herself:

 Collection, #1240 (Miscellaneous) | When she was lost in worries, watching the treetops toss:

吹き払ふ四方の木枯心あらば憂き身を隠すくまもあらせよ

Blowing from all sides,	*fukiharau*
wintry, tree-withering wind:	*yomo no kogarashi*
if you have a heart,	*kokoro araba*
open a rift in the clouds	*ukimi o kakusu*
in which to hide my wretched self.[19]	*kuma mo araseyo*

---

17. The tributes agree. *SNKS* (1:147) and *NKBT* (134) are also as above. *SNKZ* (1:181) begins *utatane no.*

18. The tributes agree. The three versions of the tale differ. *SNKS* (1:158) and *SNKZ* (1:192) have the same thing in line 2 but *madoinuru* in line 3. *SNKZ* 1 ends with *wa*, not *ni*. *NKBT* (142) has *kokoro zo itodo* and *mayowaruru* in lines 2 and 3.

19. This poem varies widely, particularly in its second half. *OMS Collection* and the three versions of the tale have *ukina* in line 4; see *SNKS* (1:174), *SNKZ* (1:210), and *NKBT* (154). *KKT* has *ukiyo* in the

POEM 19: SAGOROMO

Contest, Round 70 | When the Second Princess was feeling ill and he went to see the Empress, with the sky clouded over and drizzling as leaves fell one after another:

Collection, #375 (Winter) | Composed when he was still a commoner and visited the Grand Empress of the Saga Retired Emperor, who was home from the palace and not feeling like herself as it lightly drizzled:

人知れず押ふる袖も絞るまで時雨とともに降る涙かな

Although I hide the truth,	*hito shirezu*
I fidget with my sleeves until	*osauru sode mo*
I've wrung them out.	*shiboru made*
Still they fall with the drizzle,	*shigure to tomo ni*
my tears of love for you.[20]	*furu namida kana*

POEM 20: SAGOROMO

Contest, Round 76 | Going secretly to the palace on Sanjō [*a mistake for Ichijō?*] and hearing the calls of drakes leaving the pond:

Collection, #396 (Winter) | Going secretly to Ichijō where the Second Princess lived and feeling like a drake calling as it left the pond:

我ばかり思ひしもせじ冬の夜につがはぬ鴛鴦の浮寝なりとも

I am all alone.	*ware bakari*
I will not spare a thought	*omoi shi mo seji*
for you, this winter night—	*fuyu no yo ni*
not even a passing dream	*tsugawanu oshi no*
such as drakes do not relate.[21]	*ukine nari to mo*

POEM 21: SAGOROMO

Contest, Round 32 | Watching them build a snow mountain at the rooms of the Genji Princess:

---

same line. *SNKZ* 1 and *SNKZ Contest* have *kumo ma* in line 5. *NKBT* has *kumo mo*. *SNKZ* 1 also begins differently, with *sue harau*.

    20. The tributes agree. *SNKS* (1:178) and *SNKZ* (1:215) are also as above. *NKBT* (157) has *osouru* in line 2.

    21. All seven texts agree. See *SNKS* (1:195), *SNKZ* (1:233), and *NKBT* (169). Ducks were imagined to mate for life.

Collection, #805 (Love) | Watching them build a Mount Fuji out of snow at the rooms of the Kamo Priestess:

燃えわたる我が身ぞ富士の山よただ雪にも消えず煙立ちつつ

Burning as I go,	*moewataru*
my body is out of time,	*wagami zo Fuji no*
like Mount Fuji;	*yama yo tada*
smoke keeps rising here, too,	*yuki ni mo kiezu*
despite the snow.[22]	*keburi tachitsutsu*

POEM 22: THE RETIRED ICHIJŌ EMPEROR

Contest, Round 97 | When the Kamo Priestess was still called the Genji Princess, attached to some black bamboo covered in snow:

Collection, #435 (Winter) | Given to a person who was supposed to come to the palace, attached to an icy branch of black bamboo covered in snow:

頼めつつ幾世経ぬらむ竹の葉に降る白雪の消え返りつつ

Relying on you,	*tanometsutsu*
how many nights have I passed	*iku yo henuramu*
while on bamboo leaves	*take no ha ni*
the snow continues to fall,	*furu shirayuki no*
fades, and then returns?[23]	*kiekaeritsutsu*

POEM 23: THE GENJI PRINCESS

Contest, Round 28 | On a snowy morning, in response to "how many nights have I passed / while on bamboo leaves":

Collection, #436 (Winter) | The reply [*to poem #22*]:

---

22. *OMS Collection*, *KKT*, and *SNKS* (1:202) have *yuki tsumoredomo* in line 4. *SNKZ* (1:241) and *NKBT* (174) are as above. "Fuji" puns on "no time" (*fuji*). Heian-period writers used the smoke from the then-active volcano as a metaphor for hidden love.

23. *OMS Collection* attributes the poem to the Retired Go-Ichijō Emperor; this is the former Crown Prince, with whom Sagoromo secretly competes for the affections of both the Genji Princess and the Sen'yōden Consort. *SNKZ Contest* has *tanomitsutsu* in line 1. The six remaining texts agree. See *SNKS* (2:203), *SNKZ* (2:243–44), and *NKBT* (175).

末の世も契りやはする呉竹の上葉の雪を何頼むらむ

Who would pledge love   *sue no yo mo*
until the end of time?   *chigiri ya wa suru*
Why would black bamboo   *kuretake no*
rely on the snow   *uwaba no yuki o*
piled on its upper leaves?   *nani tanomuramu*

The version in *Collection of Wind-Blown Leaves* is considerably different:

末の世も何頼むらむ竹の葉にかかれる雪の消えも果てなで

Who would rely on it   *sue no yo mo*
until the end of time?   *nani tanomuramu*
Although the snow   *take no ha ni*
resting on the bamboo's leaves   *kakareru yuki no*
has yet to finish vanishing . . .[24]   *kie mo hatenade*

POEM 24: SAGOROMO

Contest, Round 90 | Seeing a souvenir of Asukai:
   Collection, #1050 (Love) | Looking at the fan on which Asukai had written, with its traces of her tears exceedingly clear and the picture washed away, and fearing that his own tears would stream down, too:

涙川流るる跡はそれながらしがらみとむる面影ぞなき

The River of Tears—   *Namidagawa*
traces of its flow are there, *nagaruru ato wa*
but nonetheless   *sore nagara*
there is no reflection   *shigarami tomuru*
for the fishing weirs to trap.[25]   *omokage zo naki*

---

24. KKT and *SNKS* (2:204) are as above, in the second poem. The implication of this verse is that the snow will melt momentarily. The Princess may also chide her correspondent for rushing to pledge his love as a result. *SNKZ* (2:244) and *NKBT* (175) contain elements of both poems, with a different ending. That verse reads: "Why should I rely / on it until the end? / The snow resting / on the bamboo's leaves / will never last" (*yukusue mo tanomi ya wa suru take no ha ni kakareru yuki no ikuyo to mo nashi*).

25. *OMS Collection* ends *wa nashi*. This poem exploits a common pun on brushstrokes and other remnants (both *ato*). "Reflection" glosses *omokage*, here used literally: Sagoromo imagines a real reflection in the famed River of Tears. The other texts are as above. See *SNKS* (2:212), *SNKZ* (2:255), and *NKBT* (182).

Poem 25: Sagoromo

Contest, Round 78 | Upon deciding to go to Mount Kōya:

Collection, #408 (Winter) | When he was still a commoner, while on pilgrimage to Kokawa and his boat was stopped because the Yoshino River was frozen:

沸きかへり氷の下はむせびつつさもわびさする吉野川かな

They could spring to life,	*wakikaeri*
the waters smothered up	*kōri no shita wa*
beneath this ice.	*musebitsutsu*
It, too, wanders in grief,	*sa mo wabisasuru*
the Yoshino River.[26]	*Yoshinogawa kana*

Poem 26: Sagoromo

Contest, Round 50 | Saying that he was going to Mount Kōya:

Collection, #1049 (Love) | When he was still a commoner, going on a pilgrimage to Kokawa, crossing the Yoshino River he suddenly recalled Asukai, and thinking of what her feelings must have been when it was so difficult for him even to imagine diving into its depths:

浮舟の便りに行かむわたつ海のそこと教へよ跡の白波

With a drifting boat's	*ukifune no*
worth of tidings, I will go,	*tayori ni yukamu*
across the broad sea.	*watatsuumi no*
Teach me how to plumb your depths,	*soko to oshieyo*
traces of the white-capped waves.[27]	*ato no shiranami*

---

26. *OMS Collection* and *KKT* have *wabimasaru* in line 4. *KKT* also has the particle *ni*, not *wa*, in line 2. All three versions of the tale share this version of line 2 but are otherwise as above; see *SNKS* (2:248), *SNKZ* (2:296), and *NKBT* (208). Sagoromo comments on his own suppressed tears; he is on pilgrimage due to his grief over Asukai and his other lost lovers. Kōya and Kokawa were part of the same large circuit.

27. *OMS Collection* and *KKT* have *watatsumi* in line 3, perhaps because they give the word phonetically. *SNKS* (2:248–49) is as above. *SNKZ* (2:297) has *to*, not *ni*, in line 2. *NKBT* (209) has *tayori to mo min* in the same line.

Poems from Book 3 of *The Tale of Sagoromo*

POEM 27: SAGOROMO

Contest, Round 66 | After Asukai's death, at Tokiwa:

Collection, #1130 (Love) | Hearing after her death that Asukai had gone to Tokiwa and said, "If only I could / wait to see the beech-tree wood / that vowed not to change / it would seem that autumn has / come to the groves at Tokiwa":

秋の色はさもこそ見えめ頼めしを待たぬ命のつらくもあるかな

The autumn colors—	*aki no iro wa*
yes, they look just like that.	*sa mo koso mieme*
Despite our hopes,	*tanomeshi o*
life does not keep promises;	*matanu inochi no*
they only bring more grief.[28]	*tsuraku mo aru kana*

POEM 28: SAGOROMO

Contest, Round 73 | When he was still a major captain, around the time that he heard about the Ippon Princess, he wrote to the Second Princess:

Collection, #226 (Autumn) | Around the time that he heard the decree that he should marry the Ippon Princess of the Retired Ichijō Emperor, while assuming that the Second Princess had heard of it and wondering what she thought:

折れかへり起き臥しわぶる下荻の末越す風を人の問へかし

Broken so often,	*orekaeri*
springing up, then falling flat,	*okifushi waburu*
the lower reeds grieve:	*shitaogi no*
I wish that someone would ask	*sue kosu kaze o*
after the wind that bends their tips.[29]	*hito no toekashi*

---

28. The tributes agree. *SNKS* (2:52), *SNKZ* (2:63), and *NKBT* (248) have *arame* in line 2. In Japanese, the poem translated in the headnote from *Collection* reads as follows: *kawaraji to iishi shiishiba machimibaya Tokiwa no mori ni aki ya miyuru to*. See *SNKS* (1:103) and *NKBT* (100).

29. All seven texts agree. See *SNKS* (2:85), *SNKZ* (2:98), and *NKBT* (270). The Retired Ichijō Emperor is one of Horikawa's brothers; he reigned before the tale begins. Sagoromo expresses pity for the Second Princess and asks her to reciprocate.

POEM 29: THE SECOND PRINCESS

Contest, Round 23 | When [*Sagoromo*] was still a major captain, around the time when he was visiting the Ippon Princess and said that this was not what he wanted, jotted down as writing practice:

   Collection, #989 (Love) | In what circumstances could it have been, written as writing practice on a letter from the Emperor:

夢かとよ見しにも似たるつらさかな憂きはためしもあらじと思ふに

Was it, then, a dream?   *yume ka to yo*
I have known nothing like this, *mishi ni mo nitaru*
my current misery;   *tsurasa kana*
now I see that suffering   *uki wa tameshi mo*
never follows precedent.[30]   *araji to omou ni*

POEM 30: THE SECOND PRINCESS

Contest, Round 31 | When there was "the wind that bends their tips" [*see poem #28*]:

   Collection, #228 (Autumn) | In the margin of his letter:

憂き身には秋ぞ知られし荻原や末越す風の音ならねども

Piercing my body,   *ukimi ni wa*
the autumn makes itself known. *aki zo shirareshi*
Oh, field of reeds,   *ogihara ya*
although the wind that bends your tips *sue kosu kaze no*
makes no sound as it passes. . .[31] *oto naranedomo*

POEM 31: THE SECOND PRINCESS

Contest, Round 15 | After "the wind that bends their tips" [*see poem #28*]:
   Collection, #227 (Autumn) | In the margin of this letter:

---

30. All seven texts agree. See *SNKS* (2:87), *SNKZ* (2:100), and *NKBT* (272). Reflecting on the previous poem, the Second Princess insists on the unrivaled difficulty of her life.

31. This seems to be another particularly unstable verse. *KKT* and *SNKS* (2:87) have *shiraruru* in line 2. *SNKS* 2 also has the particle *mo*, not *zo*, in the same line. *SNKZ* (2:101) and *NKBT* (272) have *mi ni shimite aki wa shiriniki* for lines 1 and 2. Like *OMS Collection*, *SNKZ* and *SNKS* list another poem by the same character (#31 here) before this one.

下荻に露消えわびし夜な夜なもとふべきものと待たれやはせし

Those nights upon nights,	*shitaogi ni*
when the dew died miserably	*tsuyu kiewabishi*
on the lower reeds—	*yona yona mo*
was it really waiting there,	*toubeki mono to*
expecting someone to come?[32]	*matare ya wa seshi*

POEM 32: ASUKAI

Contest, Round 37 | Written on a pillar in the house in Tokiwa:

　Collection, #1129 (Love) | Perhaps because she recalled the Emperor having sworn his love "on Mount Tokaeru," written on a pillar when she was living in Tokiwa:

言の葉をなほや頼まむはし鷹のとかへる山はもみぢしぬとも

I will still rely	*koto no ha o*
on the leaves of his words—	*nao ya tanomamu*
even if the trees	*hashitaka no*
on Mount Tokaeru, where hawks dwell,	*Tokaeru yama wa*
change their colors in autumn.[33]	*momiji shinu to mo*

POEM 33: ASUKAI

Contest, Round 77 | In Tokiwa:

　Collection, #1387 (Miscellaneous) | When she was in Tokiwa, not feeling like herself, written on the pillar by which she always sat:

なほ頼む常盤の森の真木柱忘れな果てそ朽ちはしぬとも

I still trust in you,	*nao tanomu*
true pillar of cypress	*Tokiwa no mori no*
in Tokiwa Grove.	*makibashira*
Do not end forgetting me,	*wasure na hate so*
even if you finally rot.[34]	*kuchi wa shinu to mo*

---

　32. *OMS Collection* and all three versions of the tale have *no* rather than *ni* in line 1; see *SNKS* (2:87), *SNKZ* (2:101), and *NKBT* (272). As noted above, *SNKS* and *SNKZ* give this poem before #30 in my collection. Here the Second Princess questions the premise of Sagoromo's letter: that they were ever in a romantic relationship. She compares herself to the dew, which evokes her tears and symbolizes a short life.

　33. The tributes agree. *SNKS* (2:128–29) is also as above. *SNKZ* (2:143) ends in *shinuran. NKBT* (299) ends line 4 with *mo*. Mount Tokaeru was famous for its fall foliage, which poets often used as a counterpoint for their steadfast affections.

　34. *OMS Collection* does not specify that Asukai is a character in *Sagoromo*. Here she asks the pillar to be more faithful than her lover (who is actually looking for her). *SNKZ Contest* opens with *na*

Poem 34: Sagoromo

Contest, Round 88 | On the day of the purification ritual for the Kamo Priestess:

Collection, #480 (Shrine Poems) | On the day of the purification ritual for the Kamo Priestess, listening to an official conduct the lustration and finding it awesome:

みそぎする八百万代の神も聞けもとよりたれか思ひ初めてし

You myriad gods	*misogi suru*
who purify the world,	*yao yorozu yo no*
listen to me now:	*kami mo kike*
who was the first of us	*moto yori tare ka*
to fall in love with her?[35]	*omoisometeshi*

Poem 35: Sagoromo

Contest, Round 75 | At the Saga Retired Emperor's villa, in the rooms of the Cloistered Princess:

Collection, #1266 (Miscellaneous) | While finding the world hateful, watching the moon set undimmed:

待てしばし山の端めぐる月だにも憂き世に我をとどめざらなむ

Please wait for a while,	*mate shibashi*
moon traveling along	*yama no ha meguru*
the mountain crest!	*tsuki dani mo*
Do you plan to leave me here,	*ukiyo ni ware o*
alone in this wretched world?[36]	*todomezaranamu*

---

o tanomu. *KKT* has *yashiro*, not *mori*, in line 2. The three versions of the tale are as above. See *SNKS* (2:129), *SNKZ* (2:144), and *NKBT* (299).

35. *KKT* has *kite* in line 3. *SNKS* (2:136) and *NKBT* (304) resemble each other: *SNKS* gives *shita* in line 4; *NKBT* has *ware koso saki ni omoisomeshika* in lines 4 and 5. *SNKZ* (2:151) is as above with an added *to* at the end. Sagoromo treats the Kamo God as a romantic rival, suggesting that he (the hero) loved her first.

36. Line 4 of this verse varies considerably across texts. *OMS Collection* and *KKT* have *hitori*, not *ware o*. *SNKS* (2:167) and *SNKZ* (2:185) give *shibashi*. *NKBT* (326) gives the line as *ukiyo no naka ni*.

POEM 36: SAGOROMO

Contest, Round 44 | To the Second Princess:

  Collection, #963 (Love) | When, drawing near to a woman who seemed entirely unsympathetic and not even receiving a reply, he decided to shut his heart to the whole world and sent her this in the morning:

命さへ尽きせずものを思ふかな別れしほどに絶えも果てなで

Now I realize	*inochi sae*
that even my life will not	*tsuki sezu mono o*
come to an end.	*omou kana*
All this time since we parted,	*wakareshi hodo ni*
and I have not breathed my last.[37]	*tae mo hatenade*

Poems from Book 4 of *The Tale of Sagoromo*

POEM 37: SAGOROMO

Contest, Round 13 | On the morning after his first visit to the Empress [*the daughter of the Princely Minister of Ceremonial*]:

  Collection, #836 (Love) | In the same circumstances [*as the preceding poem from another tale, that is, after secretly visiting a woman still uncertain about him*], sent the following morning:

おもかげは身をぞはなれぬうちとけて寝ぬ夜の夢は見るとなけれど

Your lovely profile	*omokage wa*
does not leave my side at all—	*mi o zo hanarenu*
although I did not	*uchitokete*
dream while sleeping next to you,	*nenu yo no yume wa*
fully relaxed.[38]	*miru to nakeredo*

---

37. The four tributes agree. *SNKS* (2:170) is also as above. *SNKZ* (2:187) has *inochi dani* in line 1. *NKBT* (327) has that and *tsukizu mo mono o* in line 2. Sagoromo compares his undying love to his continued painful existence.

38. *OMS Collection*, *SNKZ* (2:288), and *NKBT* (391) have the particle *mo*, not *zo*, thus *hanarezu*, not *hanarenu*, in line 2. *SNKS* (2:260) is as above. Sagoromo notes that he did not make love to the woman; the Buddhist altar in the room pricked his conscience.

POEM 38: SAGOROMO

Contest, Round 96 | Around the time that he first approached the Empress [*the daughter of the Princely Minister of Ceremonial*]:

    Collection, #788 (Love) | After a night with a woman who had not warmed up to him, unable to repress his longing for her, after night upon night of pining with his sleeping robes turned inside out, finding this strange even himself:

片敷きに重ねし衣うち返し思へば何を恋ふる心ぞ

This robe that I	*katashiki ni*
have piled atop itself	*kasaneshi koromo*
is turned inside out.	*uchikaeshi*
When I think of it like this,	*omoeba nani o*
what does my heart really want?[39]	*kouru kokoro zo*

POEM 39: THE GENJI PRINCESS

Contest, Round 6 | In response to the Emperor's [*poem about*] "darkened / by my tears":

    Collection, #276 (Autumn) | In response to the Emperor's [*poem about*] "the moon's brilliant light / clouded by my tears. / Even if it seeks lodging, / will its face get wet?" and his wish to show her this time, somehow, [*how he felt*]:

あはれ添ふ秋の月影袖ならでおほかたにのみながめやはする

It moves everyone,	*aware sou*
the autumn moon's brilliance.	*aki no tsukikage*
Surely you can see	*sode narade*
that it resides in the sky	*ōkata ni nomi*
and not in my sleeves?[40]	*nagame ya wa suru*

---

39. *OMS Collection* and *SNKS* (2:263) have *kasanenu* in the second line. *SNKZ* (2:290) and *NKBT* (393) are as above. Sagoromo refers back to the poem that inspired his sobriquet; see the introduction (*iro iro ni*). Heian lovers turned their robes inside out to dream of their lovers. Now that he finds himself longing for his sister's doppelganger, he questions his original desire, but the old feeling quickly reasserts itself.

40. The tributes agree. *SNKS* (2:324) is also as above. *NKBT* (433) has *sode narede* in line 3 and *to* instead of *ni* in line 4. *SNKZ* (2:356) has the same verse but reads line 3 as *sode narete*. The poem partially quoted in the (conflicting) headnotes reads as follows: "I long for you and weep, / with the moon's brilliant light / clouded by my tears. / Do your sleeves, where it should lodge / also soak its face?" (*koite naku namida ni kumoru tsukikage wa yadoru sode mo ya nururu kao naru*). See *SNKS* (2:323), *SNKZ* (2:356), and *NKBT* (433). There Sagoromo asks if the Genji Princess shares his feelings. He also

POEM 40: SAGOROMO

Contest, Round 98 | At the Kamo Festival, watching the messenger from the Inner Palace Guard:

Collection, #146 (Summer) | Composed on the day of the Festival, while watching the official sent to the Kamo Priestess from the Inner Palace Guard:

ひき連れて今日はかざしし葵草思ひもかけぬしめのほかかな

Pulled along by them,	*hikitsurete*
the heartvine grasses that today	*kyō wa kazashishi*
I put in my hair,	*aoigusa*
I find myself unexpectedly	*omoi mo kakenu*
yearning outside sacred ropes.[41]	*shime no hoka kana*

POEM 41: ASUKAI

Contest, Round 68 | In the mountain village of Tokiwa, when she thought her life was at an end:

Collection, #1034 (Summer) | When she was living secretly in Tokiwa, and she felt that her life had come to an end:

ながらへてあらば逢ふ世を待つべきに命は尽きぬ人は訪ひこず

As I lingered on,	*nagaraete*
waiting for a world where we	*araba au yo o*
might meet—if it exists—	*matsubeki ni*
my life has come to an end.	*inochi wa tsukinu*
My love does not visit.[42]	*hito wa toikozu*

---

compares himself to the moon, which can symbolize a lover's face in court verse. The Genji Princess replies by coolly reminding him that the moon is in the sky—and that his sentiment is cliché.

41. The tributes agree. The three versions of the tale have *aoi sae* in line 3; see *SNKS* (2:332), *SNKZ* (2:365), and *NKBT* (439). Sagoromo puns on the name of the heartvine plant (*aoi*), associated with the Kamo Shrine through the Heartvine Festival (*Aoi matsuri*), to justify his presence and amorous note. The *aoi* in his hair sounds like "*au hi*," a day when lovers meet.

42. *KKT* has an alternate *yo* ("night," not "world") in line 2. *SNKS* (2:364–65) is as above. *SNKZ* (2:400) and *NKBT* (461) have the particle *mo*, not *wo*, at the end of the same line. Asukai's poem, which Sagoromo reads in her diary near the end of the tale, is damning regardless. It contrasts her devotion, detailed in the first twenty-four syllables, with a blunt description of his absence. In the tale, Sagoromo reads several more of her poems in this scene and writes two in response. My sources share only this verse.

CHAPTER 3

"Sagoromo's Sleeves" and *"Sagoromo's* Skirts"

Overview

As detailed in my introduction, these songs use *The Tale of Sagoromo* to present the themes of separation-induced longing and the sorrows of travel, concerns familiar to their singers and audience. The libretti appear in *Treatise on Banquet Songs* (1301), an anthology compiled by the art's founder Myōkū, who wrote and scored both works. Both libretti contain interjections by the lead singer, echoing the songs' original vocalization in groups. I mimic their rhythmic meter, a loose seven-five beat evocative of verse. Myōkū also wrote poetry, as suggested by their titles, which create poetic series of words related to garments; the second title also puns on the phrase *"Sagoromo's* Spouse." Together, the songs create an extended reflection on separation and loss. My translation is visually more complicated than in the preceding chapters, since it distinguishes between allusions to the tale's poems (italicized phrases) and its exposition (underlining).

My base texts appear in *SZ*, which is moderately annotated and keyed to *NKBT*, although the annotators also note alternate lyrics. They rely primarily on a text held by the late Yokomichi Mario (1916–2012), a copy of the Yasuda-bon. In addition, I consulted the light annotations in Tōgo Yoshida's *Chūko kayō enkyoku zenshū* and *Enkyoku jūshichi chō*. They are based on texts once held in the National Office of Historiography (Shūshikyoku) and the library of Tokyo Imperial University, now Tokyo University. I follow *SZ*'s line breaks and its assignment of parts to leader and group. Unlike *SZ*, I present interjections (*soyoya, kono, ano*) as separate lines, to highlight the gesture to performance. I do not note minor differences in the alternate copy, other than poetic variants.

Translations

"*Sagoromo*'s Sleeves"

LEADER:

Oh, that's right—
そよや
The *tears* on the *sleeves* of those *narrow robes*,[1]
狭衣の袖の涙の
fell with the rain long ago, while time passed,
雨と旧にし昔の
and many different kinds of things that had been then,
様々なりし事態を

GROUP:

he tried to hide, but somehow, they got out;
つつむとすれどいさやさば
who could it have been that leaked them to the world?
誰かは世にはもらしけむ
From the very beginning, in *the springtime of youth*,[2]
少年の春の初めより
now then,
この
the season turned to summer, early summer,
首夏の夏に移きて
thin as a cicada's wing
蝉翼の薄き

---

1. *SZ* ties this song to three of the tale's poems: one from book 1, given in the introduction (*iro iro ni*); one from book 2, given in chapter 2 (poem 19, *hito shirezu*); and one from book 4, also given in chapter 2 (in a note to poem 39, *koite naku*). These verses involve different heroines.

2. *SZ* notes the debt to the first line of the tale, translated in my introduction. As detailed there, the line alludes to a Chinese couplet.

her *sleeves* gathering up the *iris-grass,*
袂にむすぶあやめ草の
roots floating and sinking on waves of tears,
ねにのみながれて浮き沈み
he resolved not to reveal *this muddy lovers' path.*[3]
かかる恋路と人はしらじ
<u>The loneliness of that village, deep in the mountains,</u>
太山の里のさびしさは
<u>except for the tracks of a stag the traces of visitors were rare,</u>[4]
棹鹿の跡より外の通路も
and amid the autumn scenery,
稀なる秋の気色に
<u>the flowers of despair alone bloomed in profusion,</u>
物思の花のみさきまさりて
<u>while the winter grasses, hidden at the water's edge,</u>[5]
汀隠の冬草の
wilted until they dried away, a moving death;
枯ゆく哀にいたるまで
there, among the songs of the various birds,
とりどりなる中にも
what, then, should I do, since we do not name its hue,[6]
いかにせんいはぬ色なる
<u>double-petal kerria rose, a single branch,</u>
八重疑冬の一枝を
<u>he broke off</u> in his hands, to show the feelings in his heart,
手折し心をしらせそめて

---

3. *SZ* notes an allusion to a poem from book 1, by Sagoromo: "Floating and sinking, / roots drifting on waves of tears, / the iris-grass— / although nobody knows / this muddy lovers' path" (*ukishizumi ne nomi nagaruru ayamegusa kakaru koiji to hito mo shiranu ni*); see *SNKS* (1:21), *SNKZ* (1:30), and *NKBT* (38). This poem contains several puns, the most obvious on muddy roads and lovers' paths (both *koiji*). There is also an implied pun on roots (*ne*) and weeping (*ne o naku*). The excerpted commentary in chapter 5 notes this poem; see gloss 62.

4. *SZ* notes an allusion to a line from book 3: "The loneliness of that village, deep in the mountains, was truly such that except for the tracks of a stag the traces of visitors were rare" (*miyama no sato no sabishasa wa ge ni saoshika no ato yori hoka no kayoiji mo, mare nakarikeru o*) (*NKBT* 217); see also *SNKS* (2:9) and *SNKZ* (2:17).

5. *SZ* notes an allusion to a line from book 2: "the flowers of despair alone bloomed in profusion, while the winter grasses hidden at the water's edge, seemed as if they might die at any moment" (*mono omoi no hana nomi sakimasarite, migiwagakure no fuyugusa wa, izure to naku aru ni mo aranu ni*) (*NKBT* 119); see also *SNKS* (1:127) and *SNKZ* (1:157).

6. *SZ* identifies two allusions: first, to Sagoromo's poem about his robes, translated in the introduction (*iro iro ni*); second, to a lengthy passage from the tale's famous opening scene. For details, see the excerpted commentary in chapter 5, glosses 1 through 4.

what could have gone through his mind, at this juncture,
隔なかりしいにしへも
given their shared past when nothing kept them apart?
今更いかがおぼしけむ
So then,
あの
letting that be,
さもこそあれ
how it is it possible not to admire that color?
いかでか色にもめでざらむ
<u>Well-suited to the time, his flowers and foliage,</u>[7]
折に付たる花紅葉
even when soaked in <u>frost, snow, or rain,</u>
霜雪雨にそほちても
and his unrivaled feelings, in the same old words,
えならぬ情の言種に
not that the answer was no, but <u>at Inabuchi</u>
いなにはあらずいなぶちの
<u>Falls, his emotions continued to crest.</u>
滝津心ぞさはぎまさる
Beginning at the palace, <u>they echoed</u> above the clouds,[8]
抑百敷の雲の上まですみのぼる
the various melodies that he then brought forth
品々の曲を調し
on both strings and bamboo; did another admire them?
糸竹の音にやめでけん
He found himself <u>longing for</u> those fluttering sleeves,
降る袖なつかしくしたはれて
now then,
この
let it stretch across the gap, a fleeting bridge of clouds,[9] he said, but as he rose
  from the ground—
はるかにわたせ雲の梯と浮たちしを

---

7. *SZ* notes another extended allusion to the exposition in book 1, here featuring Sagoromo's seasonal notes to the Genji Princess and the hidden passion that they reflect. That passage culminates in the reference to Inabuchi Falls, inspired by a poem given in the excerpted commentary in chapter 5; see gloss 32.

8. *SZ* notes another extended allusion to a passage slightly later in book 1, the miraculous concert mentioned in the introduction. This allusion culminates in the evocation of Amewakamiko, through Sagoromo's recollection of the god's dance. This deity is also noted in the excerpted commentary in chapter 5, which lists an alternate name for him; see gloss 37.

9. *SZ* notes an allusion to the poem from book 1 in which Sagoromo helps to summon Amewakamiko: "By the light of the / flashes of lightning I would / go to the Plain of Heaven; / let it

awesome though it was—*I will give to you*
かたじけなしや身のしろも
my robe as a substitute,[10] this *was a command,*
われぬぎきせんは勅なれば
so I must perforce accept,[11] but though he bent his head,
いともかしこしと仰ても
truly, *lavender of* *Musashi Plain*,[12]
げに武蔵野の紫の
sleeves *kin to* that would be quite dear.
ゆかりの袖やなつかしき
Well, then, in that case, am I the only one to get lost[13]
on love's path like this?
よしさらば我のみまよふ恋の路かは
In the past, as well, an example exists, in Ariwara;[14]
いにしへもかかるためしは在原の
his footsteps, so long ago, could they have been like this?
旧にし跡にやよそへけん
And then, what kind of tidings, born of what stolen glimpse
さてもいかなる垣間見の便にか
while I wait, my own life seems [to fade], he complained, but[15]
待つに命ぞとかこちても

---

stretch across the gap / a fleeting bridge of clouds" (*inazuma no hikari ni yukamu ama no hara haruka ni watase kumo no kakehashi*); see *SNKS* (1:32), *SNKZ* (1:43), and *NKBT* (46).

10. *SZ* notes an allusion to the Saga Emperor's poem from book 1 offering the hero the Second Princess: "I will give to you / my robe as a substitute, / so do not lament / that you gave the heavenly feather robe / back to him who offered it" (*mi no shiro mo ware nugikisen kaeshitsu to omoi na wabi so ama no hagoromo*). See *SNKS* (1:38), *SNKZ* (1:51), and *NKBT* (50).

11. *SZ* notes an allusion to an external poem from *Collection of Gleanings of Japanese Poems* (*Shūi wakashū*, ca. 1005) (book 9, Michitsuna's Mother): "It is a command, / so I must perforce accept— / but should someone ask, / 'Where is the warbler's home?' / what would you have me respond?" (*choku nareba ito mo kashikoshi uguisu no yado wa to towaba ikaga kotaemu*).

12. *SZ* notes an allusion to a poem by Genji in the "Young Murasaki" (*Wakamurasaki*) chapter. In *Sagoromo*, see *SNKS* (1:38–39), *SNKZ* (1:51), and *NKBT* (51). The famous verse in *Genji* reads: "Her root is unseen, / and yet I do love her so, / the kin [*yukari*] to that plant / the dews of Musashi Plain / put so far beyond my reach" (*ne wa minedo aware to zo omou Musashino no tsuyu wake waburu kusa no yukari o*). I borrow the translation from Tyler, *Tale of Genji*, 108.

13. *SZ* notes an extended allusion to a passage later in book 1, in which Sagoromo finds the Genji Princess viewing pictures from *Tales of Ise* and suggests emulating a pair of flirtatious siblings described there. Senji calls *Ise* "the Ariwara Middle Captain's romantic diary" (*Zaigo chūjō no koi no niki*). In that passage, Sagoromo recites this poem: "Well, then, in that case / let us follow in those steps / from the past and see / if I am the only one / to get lost on love's path like this" (*yoshi saraba mukashi no ato o tazune miyo ware nomi mayou koi no michi ka wa*); see *SNKS* (1:44), *SNKZ* (1:58), and *NKBT* (55).

14. The line contains a pun on the verb "to exist" (*ari*) and the surname Ariwara. Myōkū alludes to Ariwara no Narihira, the middle captain just noted.

15. *SZ* notes an allusion to a poem by Sagoromo from book 2, about the Second Princess; see poem 15 in chapter 2 (*shinikaeri*).

could it have been that <u>his memories came rushing back</u>?
猶又思や出けん
Like <u>smoke rising from the Eight Islands at Muro</u>[16]
室の八島の煙に
it never left his thoughts, her lovely profile,[17]
立もはなれぬ面影
with <u>Later Meeting Mountain so difficult to find</u>,
後瀬の山もしり難く
his heart could never move on, and thus,
すすむ心の程もなく
resenting the early parting of their lovers' robes,
はや衣々の恨みは
<u>he felt as if he were someone else</u>;[18]
我にもあらぬ心地して
he must have ceased his labors, the god
たえまやをかん葛城の
of Katsuragi,[19] for though he trusted in that vow
神の誓を憑ても
the following morning, the cypress door,[20]
明る朝の槙のとは
how painful he must have found that very circumstance.
さこそはくやしくおぼえけめ

---

16. *SZ* notes an extended allusion to a passage from book 2 in which Sagoromo recalls the sight of the Genji Princess's arm. For the related poem, also referenced here, see poem 5 in chapter 2 (*ware bakari*).

17. While *SZ* does not note it, the line alludes to a poem by Sagoromo from book 4, about the daughter of the Princely Minister of Ceremonial; see poem 37 in chapter 2 (*omokage wa*).

18. *SZ* notes allusions to two passages from book 2. Both describe his turbulent emotions after the night with the Second Princess. In *NKBT*, the first allusion reads as follows: "With Later Meeting Mountain so difficult to find, and her beauty growing so dramatically upon closer acquaintance, what must he have thought?" (*Nochise no yama mo shirigatō, utsukushiki on'arisama no chikamasari ni, ikaga oboshinaritamaiken*) (*NKBT* 130–31); see also *SNKZ* (1:174). This passage does not appear in *SNKS* (see 1:141–42). The second allusion reads: "In his heart, filled with increasingly tangled emotions, he felt as if he were someone else; he was increasingly frustrated" (*samazama ni midare masarinuru kokoro no uchi, ware ni mo arazu modokashiki koto kagiri nashi*) (*NKBT* 131); see also *SNKZ* (1:175). *SNKS* remains notably different but is closer here (see **1:142**).

19. *SZ* notes an allusion to a poem by Sagoromo from book 2: "That bridge of stone / if only I could cross it / night after night / he must have ceased his labors / the god of Kazuragi" (*iwabashi o yoru yoru dani mo watarabaya taema ya okan Kazuragi no kami*); see *SNKS* (1:143), *SNKZ* (1:176), and *NKBT* (132). The god of Mount Kazuragi (also written Katsuragi) was famous for failing to complete a stone bridge to the next mountain, in part because he would only work at night. Here Sagoromo tells the Second Princess, with whom he has spent the night, that he longs to see her again—but that it will be difficult. She does not reply.

20. *SZ* notes an allusion to another poem by Sagoromo from book 2, about the Second Princess: "Painful though it is, / the cypress door between us / has opened up. / I should have let things stay / as they were to begin with" (*kuyashiku mo aketekeru kana maki no to o yasurai ni koso arubekarikere*); see *SNKS* (1:144), *SNKZ* (1:177), and *NKBT* (132). Sagoromo refers to the assault.

Was it then a dream? I have known nothing like this, my current misery;[21]

夢かとよ見しにもあらぬつらさ哉

would that there might *open a rift in the clouds in which to hide my wretched self,*

うき名を隠阿もあれせよとぞ思ふ

wintry, tree-withering wind, if you have a heart.[22]

四方の木がらし心あらば

Since the age of gods, He planned to set aside the sakaki leaf,[23]

神代よりしめゆひ初し榊葉を

that branch beyond my reach, and so he mourned.[24]

及ばぬ枝と歎しぞ

Truly, this was a frustrating turn of events!

せめてこころやましきわざなりし

"*Sagoromo*'s Skirts"

LEADER:

Perhaps there was no other way, no means to calm his heart. In that small
carriage,[25]

おもひやるべき方やなかりし小車の

---

21. *SZ* notes an allusion to a poem by the Second Princess from book 3, written to herself; see poem 29 in chapter 2 (*yume ka to yo*). As seen there, she rejects Sagoromo's plea for sympathy (about his marriage to the Ippon Princess) to reflect on her own misery.

22. *SZ* notes an allusion to a poem but does not identify its source or author. It is again by the Second Princess, this time from book 2; see poem 18 in chapter 2 (*fukiharau*). As seen there, she longs for the late autumn gusts to tear a hole in the clouds in which she can hide. Myōkū works from the version of the poem that I translated, which *SZ* (using *NKBT*) flags as a variant.

23. *SZ* notes an allusion to another poem from book 2, this time by the Kamo God: "Since the age of gods / I have planned to set aside / this *sakaki* leaf; / therefore, who but I would dare / to pick it for himself?" (*kamiyo yori shimehiki yuishi sakakiba o ware yori hoka ni tare ka orubeki*); see *SNKS* (1:229), *SNKZ* (1:274) and *NKBT* (194). All three versions vary. The God refers to the *sakaki* tree, used in shrine-ritual, to claim the Genji Princess as his priestess. Myōkū shows Sagoromo remembering this verse. I capitalize the first letter of "he" to mark this reference to the god. For Sagoromo's belated response, see poem 34 in chapter 2 (*misogi suru*).

24. *SZ* notes an allusion to a poem from book 3, by Sagoromo: "What, then, should I do / with my feelings still set on / the *sakaki* leaf; / even though I know it is / a branch beyond my reach" (*sakakiba ni kakaru kokoro o ika ni sen oyobanu eda to omoitayuredo*); see *SNKS* (2:138), *SNKZ* (2:153), and *NKBT* (305). All of these poems are essentially the same; the last two are identical. This verse again marks Sagoromo's desire for the Genji Princess.

25. The reference to a "small carriage" (*oguruma*, which can also name carriages in general) stands out. As seen in chapter 1, Sagoromo meets Asukai only because he glimpses a priest's shaved head through the carriage's curtains. As indicated there, Senji describes a "woman's carriage" (*on-naguruma*), while the short tale also refers to a vehicle from Mount Ōhara. Presumably Myōkū's masculine, Kamakura-based audience found his label more meaningful.

he seemed to lose himself; from the beginning,[26]
我かもあらぬ初より

his deepest feelings showed there *at Asukai*.[27]
深き思は飛鳥井に
Without *even shadows where a traveler could sleep*, she reproached him, and he
やどりはつべき影し見えねばと
hid in the grasses avoiding others' eyes;[28]
みま草がくれの人目よきて
it was truly new to him, that pillow of grass.[29]
げに珍しき草枕を
How many were their meetings, layering one tryst on the next?
いくたびむすび重けん
As they grew ever closer, moved by their bond,[30]
馴ゆくままの哀に
he trusted in the future to prove his love;
行末遠くたのめをけば

---

26. This line alludes broadly to Sagoromo's first night with Asukai, characterized in the tale by his sense of disorientation. See, for example, poem 6 in chapter 2 (*waga kokoro*).

27. SZ notes an allusion to a poem by Asukai from book 1: "Stay here—even that / I cannot say. Asukai / has nothing at all, / not even shadows where / a traveler could sleep" (*tomare to mo e koso iwarene Asukai ni yadorihatsubeki kage shi nakereba*); see SNKS (1:64), SNKZ (1:83), and NKBT (70). The first and third versions are identical; the second varies slightly in the fourth line. This allusion continues into the next line of the song.

28. SZ notes an allusion to Sagoromo's reply to the previous verse: "At Asukai / I would like to see your face / as I take my rest; / but the person hiding there, / in the grasses, might object" (*Asukai ni kage mimahoshiki yadori shite mimagusa gakure hito ya togamen*); see SNKS (1:65), SNKZ (1:84), and NKBT (71). Sagoromo puns on the alternate reading of *kage*, translated as "shade" earlier; it can also mean reflection, which Sagoromo claims to see in the spring that gives Asukai her name. He also alludes to her kidnapper; Sagoromo imagines the priest hiding in the grasses beside the spring, used as fodder for travelers' horses. Myōkū makes this line allude to Sagoromo himself, signaling the hero's desire to hide the liaison from the Genji Princess.

29. SZ notes an allusion to a line from book 1: "Unaccustomed to pillows of grass, he found it a delight, and from then on, as he slipped out to see her with no concern for the late-night dews or those of dawn, his visits piled up" (*narawanu kusa no makura o mezurashi to oboshite, sono nochi wa, yoi akatsuki no tsuyukesa mo shirazu, magiretamau yona yona tsumorikeri*) (NKBT 72); see also SNKS (1:66) and SNKZ (1:85). "Pillow of grass" (*kusamakura*) names a traveler's bed and thus his nights with Asukai.

30. SZ notes another allusion to book 1: "as the Middle Captain continued to see her, he felt increasingly moved, until he found himself pledging his affection not just in passing but for all time" (*chūjō no kimi wa, minaretamau mama ni, awaresa masaritsutsu, naozari no koto ni wa arazu, yukusue made, chigirikataraitamaubeshi*) (NKBT 73–74); see also SNKS (1:68) and SNKZ (1:88).

he must have believed that theirs was a stable bond,
こはかかるべき契ぞとも
that their loving feelings were deeply matched.
さこそは思あはせけめ
I do not know where it will end, the mosquito smudge,[31]
行方しらぬ蚊遣火の
smoke drifting to what end? But setting that aside,
煙の末のとにかくに
<u>where might her worries take her</u>—and in the end,[32]
思みだるるはてもさば
on what kind of shoal would she <u>finally</u> rest?
つゐのよるせよいかならむ
Asuka River—even when I contemplate tomorrow's crossing,[33]
飛鳥河あすわたらんとおもふにも
today's hours of sunlight inspire such *longing*
けふのひるまのこひしさに
<u>that I wish to speak with you, of the dream I had;</u>
語あはせん見し夢の
that beloved profile never leaving her side,
かたはらさらぬ面影
on that morning before dawn, still darkened by night,[34]
まだ夜をこめし明ぐれの
filled with sheer confusion, the torment of it,
心まよひのくるしさを

---

31. *SZ* notes an allusion to poem 6 in chapter 2 (*waga kokoro*).

32. *SZ* notes an extended allusion to a passage from book 1. The tale relates Asukai's growing anxiety over her wetnurse's plan to leave the city and Sagoromo's attempts to comfort her (unsuccessful, since she does not reveal the problem). He promises Asukai that she will see his devotion "in the end" (*tsui ni*). Myōkū uses this word to foreshadow her final "shoal" or resting place (*tsui no yoruse*), artfully referencing her attempt to drown herself. This introduces the next water-themed allusion. In the tale, see *SNKS* (1:69–70), *SNKZ* (1:89–91), and *NKBT* (74–75).

33. *SZ* notes an allusion to a poem and prose fragment from book 1, mistakenly assigned to Asukai. They actually belong to Sagoromo. The poem reads: "Asuka River— / even when I contemplate / tomorrow's crossing, / today's hours of sunlight / make me long for you the more" (*Asukagawa asu wataran to omou ni mo kyō no hiruma wa nao zo koishiki*); see *SNKS* (1:98), *SNKZ* (1:124), and *NKBT* (96). Sagoromo tells Asukai that he cannot visit that night; there is a directional taboo. He wants the figurative river between them to dry up, making visits easier; *hiruma*, daylight, also means "while it dries." The prose varies notably here.

34. This passage alludes in general terms to Asukai's departure for what she thinks is a relative's home; her nurse has told her that a temporary taboo requires them to relocate. Instead, she finds herself in a carriage headed for the port. Right before this, she recalls the verse just noted, which now resonates ironically. See *SNKS* (1:104–5), *SNKZ* (1:131–32), and *NKBT* (101–3).

she wondered, should she tell *the rooster wearing mulberry floss?*[35]

ゆふつけ鳥にや言伝ん

As she hesitated there, at the heavenly door,[36]

やすらひかねし天の戸

the day <u>opened with dawn and forced them apart</u>;

明ぬといそぐ別路に

she boarded a boat, on the Yodo River;

淀の河舟さしうけて

with the oar-straps cut, my life is also cut short—[37]

梶をたえ命も絶と

how could she convey to him, from that great distance,

いかでしらせんはるばると

the many salt-water waves through which she had to pass?

いくへの浪をかわけすぎん

Wearing out her heart with love brought only sorrow.

心づくしのはてぞうき

Hearing for the first time then, of strange *Mushiage,*[38]

いまぞきくまだわがしらぬむしあげの

its roiling waves across the vast sea,[39]

浮津の浪はわたづ海の

and seeing the seaweed but sadly no chance to meet,

みるめかなしくおもふにも

<u>she had only his fan for a souvenir,</u>[40]

君がかたみに扇の

<u>which she kept beside her although it renewed her grief;</u>

名残も惜く身にそへて

---

35. *SZ* notes an allusion to a poem from book 1; see poem 9 in chapter 2 (*ama no to o*). As seen there, Asukai composes it as her nurse hustles her onto the carriage bound for the port.

36. The "heavenly door" references both the sunrise and the door of Asukai's house, at which she hesitates. *SZ* also notes an allusion to the nurse's speech hurrying Asukai along, referenced above.

37. *SZ* notes an allusion to another verse by Asukai; see poem 10 in chapter 2 (*kajio tae*). Myōkū paraphrases the rest of it in the following lines, which describe her desire to inform Sagoromo of her plight and the tears she sheds as she realizes how hard it will be to escape.

38. *SZ* notes an allusion to a poem from later in book 1, again by Asukai: "Even if I drift, / I can hope that there will be / another meeting shoal. / I take a leap of faith / into Mushiake Strait" (*nagarete mo ause ari ya to mi o nagete Mushiake no seto ni machi kokoro mimu*); see *SNKS* (1:121), *SNKZ* (1:151), and *NKBT* (114). She plans to drown herself there. As my translation of the preceding poem suggests, the place name is also read "Mushiake."

39. This section also recalls Sagoromo's poem about the Yoshino River, written while seeking Asukai; see poem 26 in chapter 2 (*ukifune no*).

40. *SZ* notes an allusion to an extended passage from book 1, which describes Asukai's feelings as she looks at the fan noted earlier, now at her pillow; see *SNKS* (1:122), *SNKZ* (1:152), and *NKBT* (114–15).

then, believing it the end, she wrote, *weeds at the*
いまをかぎりとはやき瀬の
bottom of this rapid strait,[41] beside his verse;
底のみくづと書つけし
she had no recourse but to trust the sea *breezes*
其浦かぜのつてまでも
and somehow these tidings must have found their way to him.
いかなる便にしられけん
Then even the traces of her became very dear,
なき跡までもむつましく
for visiting her house, he found a *true pillar of cypress,*
尋しやどのまきばしら
do not end forgetting me, words she had spoken;
忘れなはてそといひけるも
was this the only memento of love that would not *rot*?[42]
是や朽せぬ記念ならむ
The *seed he had planted* and left, the maiden *pine,*[43]
種まきをきし姫小松
finally grew tall, its color began to show;
つゐに木だかき色見えて
could the green of the treetops, tinged with resentment,
緑さかふる梢は
have been raised to these heights there, in *Tokiwa Grove*?[44]
常葉の森にやそ立けん

---

41. *SZ* notes an allusion to Asukai's poem in the passage just referenced; see poem 13 in chapter 2 (*hayaki se no*). As noted there, Asukai adds this poem to Sagoromo's fan just before she prepares to jump into the sea.

42. *SZ* notes an allusion to a poem by Asukai from book 3; see poem 33 in chapter 2 (*nao tanomu*). As noted there, she writes it on a pillar.

43. Here Myōkū alludes to two poems. The closer in terms of previous lines is Asukai's poem from book 4, from her diary: "Unable to trust / in the future, with my life / now at its end, / I am parted from the pine / newly rooted on the rocks" (*yuku sue o tanomu to mo naki inochi ni te mada iwane naru matsu ni wakaruru*); see *SNKS* (2:364), *SNKZ* (2:400), and *NKBT* (460). The pine refers to Asukai's daughter; the verse puns on its location and Asukai's failure to tell Sagoromo of her pregnancy (both *iwane*). However, Senji also refers to the Second Princess's son as a pine, in a verse by the Saga Empress from book 2: "May it grow until / it pierces the clouds! / He who planted the seed does not / seek the young pine on the peak" (*kumoi made oinoboranamu tane makishi hito mo tazunenu mine no wakamatsu*); see *SNKS* (1:181), *SNKZ* (1:219), and *NKBT* (159). The dying Empress wants her grandson to grow tall and strong, like a pine, despite his negligent father. In this way, Myōkū evokes the grief of both women. He also links Asukai and the Second Princess, who bear the hero's children in hard circumstances.

44. *SZ* notes an allusion to another poem by Asukai, from book 3: "Tokiwa Grove— / the place on which I had / come to rely! / Now I see that we rely / on its name, not its substance" (*tanomekoshi izura Tokiwa no mori ya kore hito tanome naru na ni koso arikere*); see *SNKS* (2:128), *SNKZ* (2:143), and *NKBT* (299). Like poem 32 in chapter 2 (*koto no ha o*), it appears on a pillar.

As time passed and he later realized the truth,
世々経て後にしられつつ
what layered fresh grief on grief ultimately was
哀をなをもかさねしは
the *crane's-down robes* at the *marsh's* edge;[45]
沢辺の鶴の毛ごろも
even so, truly, how did someone write these things and float them through
the world?
よしやげにさのみはいかが書ながさむ
Mere flowers of words leaking from the fishing *weirs*,[46]
詞の花の梁にもるる
her brushstrokes could not replace the water-reed itself,[47]
水茎の跡も及ばねば
and so, though their words had been as lush as summer grass,
夏草のしげき言の葉の
these could not preserve even a dewdrop's worth of life.
露をもみがく事なかれ
All of these things, therefore—would you not say?—
此等やさば狭衣の
make Sagoromo memorable: end, spouse, and skirts.[48]
忘られがたき妻ならむ

---

45. *SZ* notes an allusion to a poem by Asukai from book 4, written in her diary: "I hide the truth / about the inlet in the marsh; / there is no one to / hear her cries here as I wrap / the young crane within downy robes" (*hito shirenu irie no sawa ni shiru hito mo naku naku kisuru tsuru no kegoromo*); see *SNKS* (2:359), *SNKZ* (2:395), and *NKBT* (457). *SZ* contains a small error (*hitoe* for *irie*). Asukai refers to her daughter, swaddled in the white cloth used for newborns. Sagoromo compares the Second Princess's son to a crane; for this poem, see my notes to the play in chapter 4 (*shirazarishi*). Myōkū again likely intends both allusions, to heighten the song's pathos as it ends.

46. This line alludes to a poem by Sagoromo from book 2; see poem 24 in chapter 2 (*Namidagawa*). As noted there, Sagoromo looks at his fan, now bearing Asukai's poem about Mushiage/Mushiake Strait, and mourns her; the fan shows her "River of Tears," but the weir did not hold Asukai herself. While Myōkū uses a different term for weirs (*yana* rather than *shigarami*), the same conceit applies.

47. This line puns on *mizuguki* ("brushstrokes" and "water-reed") to compare Asukai's poem on the fan to the woman herself.

48. The last line puns on three meanings of *tsuma*: "skirt," echoing the imagery in "*Sagoromo's Sleeves*"; "spouse," echoing the content of "*Sagoromo's Skirts*"; and "ending," marking the conclusion to the song or combined songs in performance.

CHAPTER 4

Sagoromo

Narrow Robes

Overview

As detailed in my introduction, this play uses *The Tale of Sagoromo* to present the themes of longing, memory, and past glory, with a particular emphasis on courtly garments. It was written by the prominent courtier Sanjōnishi Sanetaka at the request of shogun Ashikaga Yoshihisa, and performed twice in 1503, after playwright Kanze Nobumitsu scored it. Like the short narratives, *Sagoromo* relies on one subplot from the tale, this time involving the Second Princess. The title is ambiguous, since the hero does not appear on stage. Plays about *The Tale of Genji* often take their names from emotionally charged images: for example, the half-shutters (*hajitomi*) on a heroine's house, discussed below (in a note to a line from the play) and in a gloss from the commentary excerpted in my final translation. Similarly, Sanetaka probably invokes the poetic term for clothing, also favored in banquet song, rather than a particular character. My translation of the title reflects that judgment.

My base text appears in *KYS*. This lightly annotated text reprints the version found in the 1914 text of the same title published by Shibunkan. I do not know its provenance. I have also consulted the version found in *NMZ*. It comes from *Bangai yōkyoku gojūichiban*, where it is classed as a third-category play: that is, a play about a woman. This would further tie the title to the

poetic trope noted above, rather than to the hero. I identify differences be-
tween the alternate libretti in my notes. Following those works, I also mark
styles of chant. I do not translate the names for those styles or for the actors'
roles; the searchable glossary at the-noh.com provides a useful starting point
for interested readers. As before, I attempt to replicate poetic rhythms, inter-
mittent uses of seven-five meter. As in the banquet songs, I italicize poetic
allusions and underline the few expository fragments from the tale. Sanetaka
also alludes to sutras. I put these phrases and those from texts other than
Sagoromo in quotation marks.

Translation

Dramatis personae

A COURT OFFICIAL (*WAKI*)

THE GHOST OF THE SECOND PRINCESS (*SHITE*)

AMEWAKAMIKO (*TSURE*)

Waki:

SHIDAI

On Saga's slope, where my Lord no longer comes,[1]
みゆき絶えにし嵯峨の山
on Saga's slope, where my Lord no longer comes,
みゆき絶えにし嵯峨の山
I will seek out the ancient, thousand-year-old path.
千代のふる道を尋ねん

KOTOBA

I am a retainer in the service of the current emperor.
これは當今に仕へ奉る臣下にて候
With autumn already half spent, I have decided to seek out
秋も半ばなり候程に

---

1. *KYS* lists an allusion to a poem in *Later Collection of Japanese Poetry* (*Gosen wakashū*, 951) (Mis-
cellaneous, Ariwara Yukihira): "On Saga's slope, / where my Lord no longer comes, / at Seri River /
still there are traces of the / ancient, thousand-year-old path" (*Saga no yama yuki no furumichi ato mo
nashi*). I adapt the translation from Carter, *Haiku before Haiku*, 119.

the colors of the meadow-flowers on the Saga plains,[2]
嵯峨野の原の花の色
and of the treetops on those western slopes.
西山もとの梢をも尋ねばやと存候

UTA

Like a jewelry box, the past opens again, Horikawa grows clear,[3]
玉くしげ再び澄める堀川の
like a jewelry box, the past opens again, Horikawa their home,
玉くしげ再び澄める堀川の
its waters flow beneath the bridge, as I cross over it,
水行く橋を打ち渡り
those traces, fondly recalled, of Momozono,[4]
跡なつかしき桃園の
and spring there—now, as in the past, exudes divinity.
春や昔に神さぶる
Passing through Uchino, beyond the sacred ropes,[5]
しめの内野を打過ぎて
truly, it is in the west, that one most feels the fall;[6]
西こそ秋と同じ身も
deeper there than anywhere the colors of the leaves,
餘處より深き紅葉はの

---

2. The hills west of the capital were known for their foliage, also noted by Senji; see poems 27 and 32 in chapter 2 (*aki no iro wa* and *koto no ha o*).

3. "Jewelry box" (*tamakushige*) is poetically tied to "again" (*futatabi*), due to a pun on the word for lid (*futa*). Sagoromo's father is known as Lord Horikawa because he lives at the intersection of Second Avenue and Horikawa Avenue, which faced the old Horikawa ("Dug River") Canal. I signal a possible pun between "to grow clear" and "to reside" (both *sumu*) in my translation.

4. *KYS* notes that Momozono is located to the north of First Avenue and to the west of Ōmiya Avenue. This part of the capital was technically outside of the city limits; see Li, *Ambiguous Bodies*, 67–69. Perhaps as a result, the estate (held by the Fujiwara family before being converted to Sesonji Temple) reportedly hosted several uncanny events. In addition to tracing the journey west from the capital to Saga, the playwright uses this landmark to borrow this otherworldly ambience.

5. *KYS* identifies Uchino as the western portion of the capital south of Ichijō Avenue, where the palace compound once stood.

6. *KYS* lists an allusion to a poem in *Continued Collection of Ancient and Modern Japanese Poems* (*Shoku kokin wakashū*, 1265) (Autumn, Minamoto Sukehira): "Even knowing that / the shadows deepen and spread, / I find that in autumn / the west seems to grow clear / along with the moon's bright light" (*wakite nao fukeyuku kage no sayakeki wa nishi koso aki to tsuki ya sumuramu*). Sukehira contrasts fall's lengthening nights with its famous moon, implicitly compared to the Buddhist paradise in the Pure Land.

I seek them out, for there is nothing that compares.
類あらしを尋ねん
I seek it out, the Mountain of Storms.[7]
嵐の山を尋ねん

KOTOBA

Since I have hurried,
急ぎ候程に
I have already arrived at the temple at Saga.
是は早嵯峨の院に着きて候
I think that I will rest here for a while,
此處に暫く休らひ
calmly reciting verse on colorful plains and slopes.
野山の色をも心静に詠めばやと存候

Shite:

"If someone with a confused and distracted mind should take even one flower
若人散亂心乃至一華
and offer it to a painted image, in time he should come to see countless
   buddhas."[8]
供養於依僧せんけん無衆佛
How wonderful this marvelous verse!
有難の妙文やな

UTA

"When I take them up, although I have defiled them with my hands,
折取ればたぶさにけがる立てながら
I offer them to the buddhas of the Three Worlds, the flowers."[9]

---

7. That is, Arashiyama, located to the west of the city. The playwright breaks this name into its literal components, *Arashi no yama*, to echo part of the previous line: in my translation, "there is nothing" (*araji*, literally, does not exist).

8. *KYS* notes a quotation from the Lotus Sutra but does not supply it. It comes from the "Expedient Means" chapter. I borrow the translation from Watson, *Lotus Sutra*, 40.

9. *KYS* explains that the *shite* essentially quotes a poem from *Later Collection of Japanese Poetry* (Spring, Sōjō Henjō). The playwright inverts the order of the last two words; Henjō gives *hana tatematsuru* and uses an alternate first line (*oritsureba*, as opposed to *oritoreba*, seen above). Janet Goff

三世の佛に奉る花の

Myriad plants, various colors—

千種も色々の

the Saga plains are suddenly a garden,[10]

嵯峨の尾やがて庭なれば

the Saga plains are suddenly a garden,

嵯峨の尾やがて庭なれば

and the Ōi River, too, is very close.

大井の川も程近く

Mount Ogura's bamboo grass and pampas grass[11]

小倉の山の篠薄

are faintly visible, and the call of the deer, too,

仄に見えて鹿の音も

cries out, to the point of pain, my own feelings.

同じ心に鳴きつくす

Evening at the lonely palace, alas,

淋しき宮の夕かな

evening for the lonely Princess, alas.[12]

淋しき宮の夕かな

Waki:

KOTOBA

This woman chanting sutras,

是なる女人の經を讀誦し

picking flowers, and lingering here

花を手折りて立休らふは

seems very purposeful in her actions.

如何様由ありげに見えて候

---

notes a nearly identical allusion near the beginning of the Noh *Hajitomi*. There the *shite* (the spirit of Genji's lover Yūgao or of the flower that inspires her sobriquet) quotes the end correctly but gives another variant of the first line: *te ni toreba*, "once held in the hand." To emphasize that echo, I base my translation of the related lines on Goff's. As she explains, the three worlds in question are the past, present, and future. See Goff, *Noh Drama*, 102–4 and 111–14.

10. As noted, Saga is famous for its foliage. Sanetaka sets the play at the site of Sagoromo's final meeting with the Second Princess; this is where the tale ends. By referencing a garden, he also reminds readers of the tale's beginning; see my introduction.

11. The reference to Mount Ogura recalls Nison-in, Sanetaka's family temple as well as Teika's villa. The commentary excerpted in chapter 5 mentions this temple specifically; see gloss 35.

12. I signal the shift in subject from the place to the Princess (both *miya*).

I will approach and ask her reasons.

立ちより尋ねばやと存候

That is something that I must ask of her.

如何にあれなる女性に尋ぬべき事の候

Shite:

Do you have business in this place?

此方の事にて候か

Waki:

Looking out we see the plains, many colors,

見れば野ももせの色々に

but "the flowers, among all flowers," "if true to their name,"[13]

花こそ花の名にしおはば

have five hindrances, I hear,[14]

五の障あるときこえ

and although I therefore left behind, the maiden flowers' blooms,

女郎花の花をすきてしも

you break them off as flowers for the Buddha;

佛の花と折り給ふは

I suppose that you have a reason for doing that?

如何なる謂れのあるやらん

Shite:

That is correct.

さん候

Long ago, when the Sagoromo Emperor

むかし此院にさごろもの御門

---

13. *KYS* notes an allusion to the beginning of the tale, in which the hero quotes from this line when giving flowers to the Genji Princess. There the season is summer. For a related poem, see the excerpted commentary in chapter 5, gloss 9 (*niou yori*). *NMZ* does not include the phrase *hana no*.

14. This notion, found in many Buddhist writings, holds that five things keep women from enlightenment. As *KYS* notes, these obstacles are the inability to become a brahma, a shakra, a devil king, a wheel-turning king, or a buddha. As noted in chapter 1, the Lotus Sutra refutes this by showing a female figure known in Japan as the Dragon King's daughter gaining enlightenment almost instantly (but she assumes a male body first).

visited this hermitage:

行幸の時

It is hard to leave without picking one of you, oh maiden flowers—

立歸りをらで過ぎうき女郎花

KOTOBA

I will linger for a while by the foggy rustic fence—[15]

なほやすらはん霧の籬にと

he composed a verse. Afterward, its traces stayed;

詠め給ひし其跡の

the flowers by that rustic fence, true to their name,

籬の花の名にしおふ

invite us "only to pluck them." Now look![16]

をれる計りと御覧ぜよ

Chorus:

RONGI

How strange! Now from a distant world,

ふしぎやさても遠き世の

wearing a narrow robe grown faded with time,

その狭衣のうらぶれて

someone prays at the grave, in the grasses' shade.[17]

跡とぶらふは草の陰

She must be kin to it, like the dew.[18]

露のゆかりの人やらん

---

15. As *KYS* notes, the *shite* quotes a poem by Sagoromo from the end of the tale, discussed briefly in my introduction: "It is hard to leave / without picking one of you, / oh maiden flowers— / I will linger for a while / by the foggy rustic fence" (*tachikaeri orade sugi uki ominaeshi nao yasurawan kiri no magaki ni*); see *SNKS* (2:373), *SNKZ* (2:410), and *NKBT* (466). The annotators of the play quote a different last line: "disoriented by fog" (*kiri no magire ni*). In both cases, the fog refers to Sagoromo's uncertainty about what to do next—and, perhaps, about which lines (fences) he can cross.

16. *KYS* notes an allusion to another poem by Sōjō Henjō, this one from *Collection of Ancient and Modern Japanese Poems* (Autumn): "I plucked you only / because your name entranced me / oh maiden flower / please do not tell all the world / that I have broken my vows" (*na ni medete oreru bakari zo ominaeshi ware ochiniki to hito ni kataruna*) (trans. Rodd, *Kokinshū*, 112). The playwright borrows the second line (*oreru bakari [zo]*) of the original verse.

17. *Kusa no kage* ("in the grasses' shade") suggests a gravesite. "Dew," a symbol of evanescence, is poetically related to grass. It also suggests a "slight" connection (*tsuyu no*).

18. On "kin" (*yukari*), see my notes to "*Sagoromo's Sleeves*" in chapter 3.

Shite:

"Kin"—yes, perhaps, but
ゆかりとも
we do not name its hue, the maiden flower.[19]
いはぬ色なる女郎花
On the withered autumn plain,
しをれはてたる秋の野の
humiliating, these sleeves of grass![20]
草の袂は羞かしや

Chorus:

"That you do not speak means more than any words"—[21]
いはぬは云ふに勝るとは
then, there on your sleeves, those glistening drops of dew, at least do not
    hide them, from a stranger's eyes.
袖のよそめにしら露のさのみなつつみ給ひそ

Shite:

Well then, in that case, I will give my name. "Nightingales,
よしさらば今は名のらん郭公

Chorus:

sing out, it is the Fifth Month"[22]—above the clouds,
鳴くや五月の雲の上

---

19. *KYS* notes an allusion to poem 1 in chapter 2 (*ika ni semu*). It refers to Sagoromo's passion for the Genji Princess.

20. The Second Princess refers to her age (as a ghost) and to her former nun's garments, so unlike the gorgeous robes of her youth.

21. *KYS* notes an allusion to a poem from *Genji*'s "Safflower" (*Suetsumuhana*) chapter: "That you do not speak / means far more than any words— / that I know full well, / yet your taciturnity / has been a hard trial to bear" (*iwanu o mo iu ni masaru to shirinagara oshikometaru wa kurashikarikeri*) (trans. Tyler, *Tale of Genji*, 120).

22. *KYS* notes an allusion to a poem from *Collection of Ancient and Modern Japanese Poems* (Love, Anonymous): "When nightingales sing / in the iris-grass / of the Fifth Month I / am unmindful of the warp / on which we weave love's pattern" (*hototogisu naku ya satsuki no ayamegusa ayame mo shiranu koi mo suru kana*) (modified from Rodd, *Kokinshū*, 183). Sanetaka borrows the first two lines (*hototogisu naku ya satsuki no*) of the original verse. While *KYS* does not mention it, the initial phrase recalls Sagoromo's playful verse about *Tales of Ise* also evoked in "*Sagoromo*'s Sleeves"; see my notes to chapter 3 (*yoshi saraba*).

that flute of jointed bamboo formed an excuse
其笛竹のかごとにて

to trade my worthless self for a night's melody;
一夜の節も数ならぬ

offered as *his personal robe, a substitute*[23]
身のしろ衣たちかへて

for heavenly sleeves, they became nun's sleeves, wasted.[24]
あまの袂のいたづらに

They rotted away; know that I did, too.
朽ちはてし身とおぼしめせ

They rotted away; know that I did, too.
朽ちはてし身とおぼしめせ

With one loving a spouse whom no one recognized,[25]
夫おもはざるを思ひ

and the other unable to love him when he looked to her,[26]
おもふを思はず

the ordered relationship, of man and wife, was cold;
さだむるいもせの中はうとく

he yearned to pledge his love to someone forbidden,
ゆるさぬ人の契りをしたふ

but all of this was just the way of the fickle world.
皆あだしよの習ひなり

Shite:

SASHI

Long ago, when Sagoromo was still a middle captain,[27]
昔さ衣の君まだ中将と聞えしとき

---

23. *KYS* notes the allusion to another poem also used in *"Sagoromo's* Sleeves," the Saga Emperor's offer of the Second Princess; see my notes to chapter 3 (*mi no shiro mo*).

24. Sanetaka puns on "heaven" and "nun" (*ama*), foreshadowing the Princess's tonsure. A third pun on "fisherman" creates a poetic series of images related to water, evoked by reference to tear-rotted sleeves that comes next. Sanetaka uses the alternate term for sleeves, *tamoto*; this refers more narrowly to the sleeve's ends. The term recalls a relevant poem by the hero, for the Sen'yōden Consort: "Loving you so long / my sleeves are never dry / of these lover's tears, / but today it is the roots / of the iris that weep" (*koiwataru tamoto wa itsumo kawakanu ni kyō wa ayame no ne sae nakarete*); see *SNKS* (1:24), *SNKZ* (1:34), and *NKBT* (40). Sagoromo puns on tears and weeping. For the Consort's reply, see my notes to the excerpted commentary in chapter 5, gloss 69 (*uki ni nomi*).

25. That is, Sagoromo, who loves the Genji Princess.

26. That is, the Second Princess, who cannot accept Sagoromo's affections when he warms to her in private.

27. *KYS* identifies Sagoromo as the son of "the great minister (*dajōdaijin*) Kanemichi." On Kane-michi, and for more mergers of fiction and history, see chapter 5. The next section retells Amewaka-miko's descent (see the introduction).

Chorus:

during the Fifth Month with its iris-grass,[28]
比は五月のあやめ草
the peerless sound of his flute as he played[29]
ねもたぐひなく吹く笛の
called down an admiring escort from the distant
響きにめでて久堅の月の都の
moon capital.
御むかへ
He was invited to ascend to the heavens,
あまつ空にとさそひしに

KUSE

but so many imperial decrees
さまざまの御ことのり
rained down that although he longed to follow
下れば登るあま人の
the rising deity, he remained in this world.
跡をしたひて此世には
He found them hard to live within then, his narrow robes;
住み果てがたき狭衣の
for while his heart and hem were stained with love, for another,[30]
心をそむるつまにもと
a decree went out to give him
女二の宮を給はんの
the Second Princess. But
御定ありしかど
one color atop another he would not wear, though he hid the truth,[31]
色々に重ねてはきじ人しれず
it already bore love's hue, the lavender.[32]
思ひそめてき紫の
For that hue, he shattered hearts but we
色に心をくだきしに

---

28. Another allusion to the verse noted above (*koiwataru*). While Sanetaka skips the earlier episode to focus on Amewakamiko, the iris-grasses point to the hero's taste for romance.

29. *NMZ* has *mukashi*, not *ne*, at the start of this line.

30. The line contains the same poetic series of images discussed in the introduction.

31. *KYS* notes the allusion to the poem given in my introduction (*iro iro ni*). I modify my translation to suit the story-telling purpose of this section.

32. *KYS* ties the last phrase in the line to Sagoromo's formal reply to the Saga Emperor's offer, where the hero suggests that if the gift were the Genji Princess, he would accept.

Shite:

could not escape our pledge; what, *did he not know?*[33]
のがれぬ契かやしらざりし

Chorus:

The wrong that he did was lost among the reeds, the young crane's call,
蘆の迷ひのたづの音を
it lingered *above the clouds*
雲の上にもとどめおき
and once again he left. For him, this was *love's path*,[34]
又立ち歸る戀路なれど
but I saw myself as the unlucky one
身はうき物と思ひとり
and donned black robes for a bleak world, my destiny in Saga.[35]
浮世のさがに墨染の
How many nights have I passed, staring at the dusk?
いく夕暮れを眺めこし
These stories of the past are meaningless—and so,
むかし語りはよしなしと
leaving these words behind, she faded from sight;
云ひすてて見えざりき
leaving these words behind, she became lost to sight.
云ひすてて見えずなりにけり

UTA

The autumn wind, too, blows through the deepening night
秋風も深け行く夜はの
on the Mountain of Storms.[36]
あらし山

---

33. *KYS* notes an allusion to a poem from book 2 of the tale, by Sagoromo: "Not knowing the wrong / that I did lost in those reeds / the young crane calls / nor could I have guessed his cries / would reach up above the clouds" (*shirazarishi ashi no mayoi no tazu no ne o kumo no ue ni ya kikiwatarubeki*); see *SNKS* (1:199), *SNKZ* (1:238), and *NKBT* (172). *SNKZ* gives a different particle at the end of the third line. Sagoromo uses a series of plays on words to communicate his shock and feelings of guilt at fathering a child on the Second Princess. Sanetaka uses the line to let the Second Princess express her own grief.

34. The phrase again recalls the poem given in "*Sagoromo's Sleeves*," referenced above.

35. The Second Princess refers to her tonsure and subsequent life at the hermitage. Sanetaka puns on "Saga" and "destiny."

36. Sanetaka repeats the earlier reference to Arashiyama to announce a new ghost. The phrase "autumn winds, too" signals that something else is blowing: Sagoromo's flute, at least in memory. This ushers in Amewakamiko, who does not speak. Again, this reverses the tale's sequence: Senji introduces the deity before the Princess.

The autumn wind, too, blows through the deepening night
秋風も深け行く夜はの
on the Mountain of Storms,
あらし山
and the unblemished moon shines down along with it.
限なき月もてりそひて
The water, too, is green, in the Ōi River,[37]
水もみどりの大井川
and its waves carry the strains of flutes;
浪にたぐへてふえの音の
they echo across the clouds—truly, it is strange.
雲に響くぞふしぎなる
They echo across the clouds—truly, it is strange.
雲に響くぞふしぎなる
"Several specks of fading stars,
さむせいいくばくてんぞ
wild geese stretch across the passes,
關峽に横はる
one note from a long flute, a person leans from the tower."[38]
長笛一聲人樓による
The brightness of the foothills is "the same color as Heaven";[39]
さんかのしらしき長天と一色にして
"on earth or in heaven we shall surely meet again."[40]
天上人間たまたまあひみる

---

37. Again, Sanetaka returns us to the beginning of the play. I am not sure what besides the water could be green. Sanetaka may mean the sky, which Senji describes as having strange clouds, noted below; see *SNKS* (1:31–32), *SNKZ* (1:42–43), and *NKBT* (45–46).

38. These lines come from "Autumn View of Chang'an," a verse by Zhao Gu (J. Chō Ka). I borrow the translation from Owen, *Late Tang*, 244. Sanetaka probably quotes a Chinese poem because Amewakamiko and Sagoromo reportedly exchange Chinese verse (not given in the tale).

39. This is an allusion to another T'ang poet, Wang Bo (J. Ō Botsu): specifically, to a popular couplet from his "Preface to 'Ascending the Gallery of Prince Teng in Hongzhou Prefecture on an Autumn Day at a Farewell Feast." The full couplet reads, "Sunset auroral cirruses scud in unison with a forlorn duck; / Autumnal waters mingle in one color with the immense sky." I borrow the translation from Chan, "Dedication and Identification," 247.

40. *KYS* notes the allusion to Bai Juyi, also evoked in the tale's opening phrase; see the introduction. This time the debt is to "The Song of Everlasting Sorrow." I borrow the translation from Bynner, *Jade Mountain*, 120. This poem laments the permanent separation of a Chinese emperor and his favorite consort, who continued to pine for each other after death. Sanetaka uses the allusion to conjure a romantic atmosphere. Since the Second Princess never loved Sagoromo, this substantially rewrites the tale. In addition to softening Senji's portrait of the relationship, Sanetaka may foreshadow the impending miracle. The emperor in "Song" sends a Daoist to find his beloved in paradise, bridging worlds as does Amewakamiko's visit.

How extraordinary, at this very moment!

あら面白の折からやな

ISSEI

As the setting moon and sunrise brighten the dark sky,[41]

夕月夜暁やみの空晴て

Chorus:

and the *lightning* flashes continuously,

稲妻の影隙もなく

the past and storm seem to meet, to play in tune.

こし方嵐吹あはすめる

The clear strains of the flute now echo close at hand.

笛の音もまぢかく聞えたり

Raising purple clouds like curtains, his hair bound up in coils[42]

紫の雲の戸張を総角の

like clouds the loops atop his head are tangled up,[43]

雲のびんづら打ち亂れ雪をめぐらす

and his sleeves circle, spitting snow.[44]

袂かな

Shite:

Amewakamiko's sleeves now dance—[45]

天稚御子の舞の袖

---

41. The following lines (four in total) mimic details from the description of the scene in the tale; see *SNKS* (1:31–32), *SNKZ* (1:43), and *NKBT* (45–46). See also the excerpted commentary in chapter 5, glosses 91–98. The reference to lightning also recalls the poem given in the notes to "Sagoromo's Sleeves" in chapter 3 (*inazuma no*).

42. This line contains a pun on "raising curtains" (*tobari o age*) and *agemaki*, an old-fashioned hairstyle used by children of both sexes that involved piling the hair into two buns, one on either side of the head.

43. Sanetaka now refers to the hairstyle by the alternate, masculine label *binzura* and implicitly compares it to the clouds. This expression also appears in the Noh *Yōkihi*, about the consort referenced earlier.

44. The sleeves (again *tamoto*) conjure romance, as does the earlier mention of tangles; it evokes tangled feelings. Together, they suggest a lovers' meeting (tangled sleeves) and its aftermath. The reference to snow, not found in the versions of *Sagoromo* noted here, returns us to the play's opening lines. The imperial journey noted there (*miyuki*) may pun on snow; see the translation in McCullough, *Kokin Wakashū*, 235. Sanetaka also marks the end of the implied romantic encounter; winter signals the end of love in court verse. The rest of the play focuses on Amewakamiko, a more auspicious figure than the Second Princess.

45. These sleeves are now *sode*, again pointing to a broader frame of reference.

they return the past to the present.

昔を今に返すなり

You who travel here from the flower capital,[46] pay close attention and
　observe what comes next.

花の都の旅人も心をとめて見給へや

Chorus:

I will give to you my robe, as a substitute; therefore, do not weep,[47]

みのしろ衣ぬぎきせむかへしつと

Shite:

over having given back

思ひな侘びそ

Chorus:

the heavenly feather robe "that brushes it so seldom

天の羽衣まれに來て

that the rocky crag itself, impervious to caress,"[48]

なづとも盡きぬ岩ほぞと

does not move, as expected. So, too, this sovereign,[49]

ためしに動かぬこの君の

his heavenly line stretches from the distant past.

あまつ日つぎの遠き世を

---

46. The "flower capital" (*hana no miyako*) is a medieval sobriquet for the imperial capital, Kyoto.
Since the word "flower" in classical poetry generally refers to springtime—and more particularly,
cherry blossoms—this reference to the imperial capital also underscores the temporary return of
life, and beauty, to the ruins of the Saga hermitage in autumn.

47. Sanetaka quotes the poem by the Saga Emperor, offering the hero his daughter. The play
omits the first-person pronoun (*ware*).

48. The phrase "heavenly feather robe" (*ama no hagoromo*) allows Sanetaka to pivot between
two literary contexts at the play's emotional climax. Initially, the phrase refers to Amewakamiko
and the verse just noted. KYS says that the phrase "heavenly feather robe" points to an anonymous
poem from *Collection of Gleanings of Japanese Poems*: in full, "my lord's life must / be a rocky craig
impervious / to the caress / of the heavenly feather robe / that brushes it so seldom" (*kimi ga yo wa
ama no hagoromo mare ni kite nazu to mo tsukinu iwaho naranamu*) (trans. Rodd, *Shinkokinshū*, 59; note
that while Rodd gives the penultimate verb as *tsukinu*, KYS has *tsuginu* in its note). As Rodd observes,
this poem refers to the Buddhist concept of a kalpa, the immense span of time required for a feather
robe to erode a giant boulder when brushing it once a millennium. For another measurement of a
kalpa, see the excerpted commentary in chapter 5, gloss 26.

49. This line invokes the conventional felicitous comparison of imperial rule, in its antiquity, to
the length of time necessary for pebbles to "grow" into giant rocks. The reference to antiquity again
echoes the play's first allusion.

Now its tutelary god, Amewakamiko, changes things back[50]
守りの神のあめわかみこの舞の袂を

with a wave of his dancing sleeves,[51]
ひるがえし

and parting the clouds again, he withdraws from sight;[52]
又雲分けて入給ふ

parting the clouds again, he withdraws from sight.
又雲分けて入給ふ

---

50. Sanetaka calls Amewakamiko a protective deity (*mamori no kami*). The libretto connects this god to the imperial line. However, Senji ties Sagoromo's accession to the imperial house's actual tutelary god, Amaterasu (see the introduction). Sanetaka seems uncomfortable with that link, as does Jōha, who implicitly ties Sagoromo's rule to the Kamo God; see the excerpted commentary in chapter 5. In the play, Amewakamiko's dance also returns us to the present. This is a comfortable distance from the hero's enthronement and its catalyst in the tale: Amaterasu's oracle, tied to his assault of the Second Princess. Sanetaka never mentions that night in her Kokiden apartments. Instead, he highlights the end and beginning of her arc: Saga and Amewakamiko's visit.

51. In this case, *tamoto*. Sanetaka's diction here would seem to refute my earlier claim about the play's expansive conclusion. The choice may be practical; this long line presents three rhythmic phrases of seven beats each. Using *sode* for sleeves would shortchange the meter. *Tamoto* also conjures a romantic attachment to the vanishing deity.

52. Strictly speaking, Amewakamiko parts the clouds and enters them. This detail differs from the tale. Senji has the god ride off in his cloud-carriage (*kumo no koshi*); see SNKS (1:33–34), SNKZ (1:45), and NKBT (47).

CHAPTER 5

Excerpt from *Sagoromo's Undersash*

Overview

As detailed in my introduction, *Undersash* is the leading commentary on *The Tale of Sagoromo*, written by linked-verse master Satomura Jōha. Since Jōha loaned out his notes while he worked, there are several competing lineages of the exegesis, just as with the cycle of short narratives and the tale itself. The versions that I have seen contain a preface and short genealogical section, followed by over a thousand glosses on Jōha's own version of the tale. The title and first line create a poetic series of images about clothing, like the banquet songs, but the keyword also hints that Jōha will expose the tale's secrets, related to politics as well as verse.

My base text appears in *SMKR*. It transcribes a text with a cover brushed by aristocrat Konoe Hisatsugu (1622–53), held by Yōmei Bunko; this copy descends from Jōha's first draft. I have also consulted another unannotated text, found in *KCS*. I do not know its source and, unlike *SMKR*, *KCS* does not number glosses. It does provide diacritical markers, useful for understanding cryptic comments. Jōha only includes phrases from his copy of the tale, now lost.

My excerpt starts at the beginning of the commentary and ends with its hundredth gloss, keying throughout to *SMKR* and the alternate text as well as the featured modern editions of the tale, cited collectively (when they present the same text) as "the series." I include the Japanese script and its transliteration for Jōha's quotations from the tale, as well as for all poems cited as intertexts. I also provide brief narrative contexts for the excerpts in my notes and identify Jōha's other sources when possible. Italics mark supplementary notes in Hisatsugu's manuscript, shown in *SMKR* by smaller print, while parenthetical phrases mark interlinear notes, perhaps added by someone else. I have italicized them, too, since they are also presumably supplemental. I supply the material given in brackets.

Translation

[Preface]

About this treatise on *Sagoromo* called *Undersash*: since many errors were re-copied even in the many tales collected near Nagara Bridge, I was asked to mark those places where the meaning seemed uncertain.[1] When I looked at the old manuscript, I found it difficult to discern either the sentiment or the language; then, after I had assisted the priests in the Fugen Hall near the pre-cincts of the Kamo Shrine in their building campaign, I saw in the bottom of a box of the Nirvana Sutra a notebook with the label "Undersash."[2]

Thinking it a gift from the god, I put it in my robes and returned home.[3] Those who understand *The Tale of the Shining Genji* do not need this trea-tise.[4] Because persons like Ichijō Zenkō and Sōgi don't take it up, lectures and the like seem to have died out.[5] The Shōyōin Lord constructed a family

---

1. This bridge evokes long spans of time and yearning; "Nagara" echoes *nagashi*, long, and *nagare*, flows of time and water, including tears. The bridge also evokes rot; it was often impassable. See the introduction for more details on this section. For additional background, see Kamens, *Uta-makura*, 118–40. Jōha refers to the tale by its abbreviated title, permitting the poetic series of images noted in the introduction. To avoid confusion with Sanetaka's play, I will reserve this term for the hero in notes to the current translation.

2. The language here reveals Jōha's poetic training and knowledge of the tale. The first half of the sentence invokes a crucial topic in *waka* poetics, the distinction between form and content. I use Kamens's translations of those terms, part of a useful discussion in *Utamakura*, chap. 1. The second half of the sentence refers to the tale's plot. The reference to the Nirvana Sutra (*Nehangyō*) evokes a medieval analogy. Like the Nirvana Sutra, Senji's tale allegedly spoke to readers not moved by an earlier, more successful text: *Genji*, paired with the Lotus Sutra. See Sudō, *Sagoromo monogatari juyō no kenkyū*, 195–223.

3. Jōha's reference to putting the manuscript "in his robes" (*kaichū / futokoro no naka*) again serves a double purpose. Several critics note that Senji stresses the special intimacy of this space by showing Sagoromo snuggling his children there. This image also shows up in illustrations; see the overlapping robes in the image from the alternate version of *The Sagoromo Middle Captain* reproduced in Nakano, *Nara ehon emakishū*, 86. By allegedly protecting the paper like this, Jōha also shows his reverence for the god's gift.

4. *Somo somo Hikaru Genji monogatari no kokoro mitokanaba, kono shō ni oyobubekarazu.*

5. Jōha suggests that the scholar Ichijō Kanera (1402–81)—here referred to by an alternate title—and *renga* master Sōgi (1421–1502) also studied the tale. Both men wrote commentaries or lectured

tree.[6] Those persons who happen to amuse themselves looking over this should continue to correct any mistakes.[7]

Copy completed in early winter of the eighteenth year of Tenshō [1590] by the novice Hansei.[8]

Family Trees for *Sagoromo*[9]

Retired Emperor Ichijō [reigned] sometime around the Chōtoku era. *The Tale of Genji* [is] a work of the Kankō era. *Chōtoku era, Chōho era, Kankō era*.[10]

Akimitsu: concurrently major captain and Minister of the Right.[11]

Lord Horikawa: in this tale, he must be Retired Emperor Enyū's second prince.[12]

Father, the Riverside Middle Counselor: *Governor of Echizen* Tametoki.[13]

---

on *Genji* and *Ise*. Kanera also allegedly wrote a lost play about *Sagoromo*, while Sōgi taught Sanetaka (noted below) *renga*.

6. Sanjōnishi Sanetaka. See the introduction.

7. *SMKR* corrects *goran ataran* to *goran aran*.

8. Jōha's signature. Like many poets, he was a lay priest. "Novice" translates *shami*; "Hansei" means "half awake" or "half sober."

9. *SMKS* specifies the reign generally when the order of succession does not follow the order of birth. *KCS* numbers every reign. The chart generally names emperors by their final title (retired emperor or *in*) unless they died in office. The exceptions, Uda and Murakami, get no formal labels at all. Uda (r. 887–97) is noteworthy for having initially been demoted to commoner status, like Sagoromo's father. There is a mistake in the reference to Murakami. Murakami (r. 946–67) was the sixty-second emperor of Japan, not the sixtieth. *KCS* (428) gives the correct number and specifies that Daigo was Uda's first prince. I will abbreviate comment on Jōha's selective use of titles other than to say that it seems deliberate.

10. Chōtoku spanned the years 995 to 999, during the reign of Emperor Ichijō. Kankō spanned 1004 to 1012, the year after Ichijō's death. The supplementary note identifies the sequence of these eras, including the intervening Chōho years for good measure.

11. This heading and the next, as well as the second family tree, are nested beneath the reference to Emperor Ichijō. Fujiwara Akimitsu (944–1021) married daughters to both Ichijō and Koichijō-in. The latter was a deposed prince, as suggested by the first family tree. According to the history *The Future and the Past* (Gukanshō, ca. 1219–20), Akimitsu blamed Fujiwara Michinaga (966–1028) for engineering Koichijō-in's retirement; see Brown and Ishida, *The Future and the Past*, 69–70. While Akimitsu eventually attained the rank of Minister of the Left, he continued to clash with Michinaga and allegedly haunted him after his death.

12. Fujiwara Kanemichi (925–77), father to Akimichi and a consort of Emperor Enyū (r. 969–84); here referred to by the name of his residence on Horikawa Avenue. For a description of the compound and a list of its successive owners, see McCullough and McCullough, *Flowering Fortunes*, 385–86. The building was allegedly one inspiration for *Genji's* Rokujō-in and the enormous estate of Sagoromo's father, also known as Lord Horikawa. The gloss identifies the character with one of Enyū's sons. This makes the fictional Horikawa the brother of Emperor Ichijō, noted earlier. In the following chart, Fujiwara Morosuke (909–60) was the grandfather of Emperors Reizei (r. 967–69) and Enyū. The two sobriquets listed for him again name estates. Fujiwara Koretada (924–72), also known as Koremasa, had a residence on Ichijō Avenue. His posthumous name means "humility." Kanemichi's posthumous title refers to his loyalty.

13. Jōha now turns to a new topic, the lineage of *Sagoromo's* author; *KCS* (429) presents this information as another family tree. Jōha mistakenly credits the tale to Murasaki's daughter, Daini Sanmi (999–1082), discussed below. This was a common view in the medieval period; see D'Etcheverry,

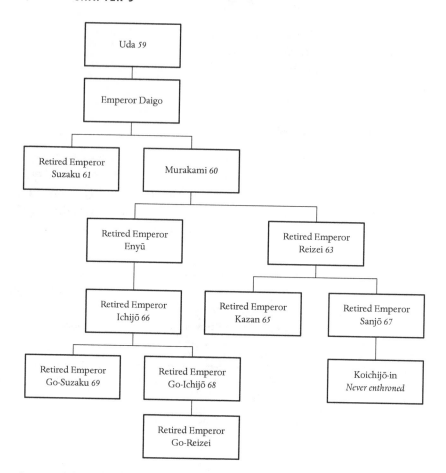

FIGURE 1. The tale's origins.

Murasaki Shikibu *author of The Tale of Genji*. She married Nobutaka, Provisional Deputy in the Ministry of the Left and gave birth to Daini Sanmi *author of Sagoromo*.[14]

This tale is a likeness of *The Tale of Genji*.[15] It resembles Major Captain Yūgiri, the Reizei Retired Emperor, and the like.[16] When the Priestly Retired

---

Love after "The Tale of Genji," 40. Fujiwara Tametoki (d. 1029), who held the office indicated in the supplementary comment above, was the father of Murasaki Shikibu. His father Kanesuke (877–933) was known as the Riverside Middle Counselor for the location of his residence.

14. *SMKR* gives an interlinear correction in the word "Genji," substituting the traditional second character in place of "father." Fujiwara Nobutaka (d. 1001?) and Murasaki Shikibu had one child, Kataiko. The sobriquet used here and in my preceding note literally means "the Assistant Governor-General of the second rank."

15. *Kono monogatari wa Genji monogatari no omokage nari.*

16. Here the name "Reizei" refers to Genji's fictional son, not the historical emperor noted earlier. In order to keep these categories clear, I refer to fictional examples as above: the Reizei (Retired)

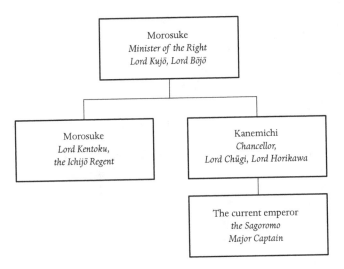

FIGURE 2.   Models for the hero and his father.

Emperor Kazan, or perhaps Emperor Uda, was still an unranked prince and chamberlain, the Kamo God appeared to him during a hunt and declared that there should be a special festival.[17] When the prince replied that he didn't know anything about it, the god asserted that there was a reason and ascended. Not long after that, completely unexpectedly, the prince became emperor, and so ever since the Eleventh Month of the first year of Kampyō [889] there has been a special festival.[18]

The era [in which *Sagoromo* was written] is unclear. *The Tale of Genji* was written during the reign of Retired Emperor Ichijō, in the Kankō era; [*Sagoromo*] was perhaps forty years later.[19] Persons who understand *The Tale of Genji* do not need this commentary.[20]

Emperor, not (Retired) Emperor Reizei. Like the fictional Reizei, Sagoromo takes the throne despite being the son of a commoner—albeit in very different circumstances. Sagoromo resembles Yūgiri, meanwhile, in his longtime rank of major captain. Jōha uses this poetic style, moving by association, throughout this section.

17. Emperor Kazan (r. 984–86) took vows upon abdicating, earning the sobriquet used above. Like Koichijō-in, he was reportedly manipulated by Michinaga. Uda, noted earlier, reigned despite having once been demoted to commoner status.

18. That is, in addition to the regular Kamo Festival referenced in the headnotes to poem 40 in chapter 2 (*hikitsurete*). This story appears in several medieval sources.

19. As noted earlier, Kankō spanned 1004 to 1012. Current wisdom holds that the tale was written later, around 1070.

20. *Genji monogatari kokoroetaran hito wa chūshaku ni oyobazaru nari.* As before, Jōha suggests that knowledge of *Genji* is sufficient to understand Senji's tale, or at least that someone who knows *Genji* will not find *Undersash* helpful.

[Entries on Book 1 of *Sagoromo*: #1–100]

(1)   the springtime of youth (*shōnen no haru* 少年の春):
This phrase comes from "treading on petals we share lamentation for the springtime of our youth." "Youth" means "the new year." This must mean stepping on flowers.[21]

(2)   the wisteria on the central island (*nakajima no fuji wa* 中嶋の藤は):

夏にこそさきかかりけれ藤花松にとのみもおもひけるかな

Now, in the summer,	*natsu ni koso*
they open, trailing down,	*sakikakarikere*
wisteria blossoms.	*fuji no hana*
Perhaps they thought that the pines,	*matsu ni to nomi mo*
pining still, would wait for them.	*omoikeru kana*

[The allusion] is just words.[22]

(3)   near Ide (*Ide no watari* ゐでのわたり):

春の池ゐでの川せにかよふらん岸の山吹そこもにほへり

Why, the lake in spring	*haru no ike*
must recall the glinting stream	*Ide no kawase ni*
of Ide River;	*kayouran*
for the kerria roses	*kishi no yamabuki*
blossom also in its depths.	*soko mo nioeri*

This is a likeness of *Genji*'s "Butterflies" chapter.[23]

(4)   the serving boy (*saburaiwarawa* 侍童):
As above.[24]

(5)   the Genji Princess (*Genji no miya* 源氏宮):

---

21. See *SNKS* (1:9), *SNKZ* (1:17), and *NKBT* (29); *KCS* (430). I again borrow the translation from Rimer and Chaves, *Japanese and Chinese Poems*; see the introduction. Jōha identifies the relevant lines. He explains *shōnen*, the tale's first word, in terms of *shinnen*, used in medieval Japanese verse.

22. See *SNKS* (1:9), *SNKZ* (1:17), and *NKBT* (29); *KCS* (430). Jōha quotes from the description of Sagoromo's garden, which has the usual pond and islets. The historical Horikawa estate was famous for its gardens. Jōha does not place the poem from the gloss. It appears in *Collection of Gleanings of Japanese Poems*. The series quote the fourth line; *SNKS* and *SNKZ* drop the last particle. Jōha asserts that there is no connection between this verse, which evokes a woman pining for her lover, and Sagoromo's situation.

23. See *SNKS* (1:9), *SNKZ* (1:17), and *NKBT* (29); *KCS* (430). Jōha again quotes from the description of the hero's garden. Ide was famous for its kerria roses. The gloss identifies an allusion to a poem from *Genji*'s *Kochō* chapter. I borrow the translation from Tyler, *Tale of Genji*, 442. Like *KCS*, Tyler's text adds the particle *ya* to the end of line 1.

24. See *SNKS* (1:9), *SNKZ* (1:17), and *NKBT* (29); *KCS* (430). Jōha points to the first action of the tale, Sagoromo's order that his page pick flowers. The gloss suggests another parallel with "Butterflies."

Sagoromo's cousin. Lady Horikawa is the younger sister of the previous emperor (*Retired Emperor Enyū*). She was the Ise Priestess. When she stepped down from this post, Horikawa took her in. She is Sagoromo's mother. Chūnagon and Chūjō are attendants of the Genji Princess.[25]

(6)　lying down (*soifusase* そひふさせ):
　　She is next to the two court attendants.[26]

(7)　the Crown Prince (*Tōgū* 東宮):
　　This is the Go-Ichijō Retired Emperor.[27]

(8)　the graceful curve of the wisteria (*fuji no shinai* 藤のしなひ):
　　This is 級字. You read it *katakudari*. It means 級照 or 片岡.[28]

(9)　whose flowers, among flowers (*hana koso hana no* 花こそ花の):
　　There must be a poem in *Ten Thousand Leaves*. Lord Teika writes:

にほふより春の暮行山吹の花こそ花の中につらけれ

Rather than their glow	*niou yori*
as spring darkens it is the	*haru no kureyuku*
kerria roses	*yamabuki no*
whose flowers, among all flowers,	*hana koso hana no*
stand out in the season's ranks.[29]	*naka ni tsurakere*

---

25. See *SNKS* (1:9), *SNKZ* (1:17), and *NKBT* (29); *KCS* (430). Jōha notes the first reference to the Genji Princess. Here Sagoromo and his page bring her the flowers that the page has just picked. The gloss concerns the Princess's attendants, described as *kyūjo* ("palace women") rather than the broader *nyōbō*. It then identifies the Princess's relationship to Sagoromo and his mother. None of the versions of the tale considered Lady Horikawa until later (see gloss 20). *KCS* assigns the supplementary comment about the Princess to the gloss and treats Lady Horikawa's relationship to the previous emperor as a supplementary comment.

26. See *SNKS* (1:9), *SNKZ* (1:17), and *NKBT* (29); *KCS* (430). I substitute the gloss from the latter version of *Undersash* (*futari no kyūjo e nari*) for a seeming error in *SMKR* (*futari no kyūjojin nari*). Jōha quotes a description of the Genji Princess as she observes Sagoromo's conversation with her attendants. The preferred version identifies where the Princess is resting.

27. See *SNKS* (1:9), *SNKZ* (1:17), and *NKBT* (29); *KCS* (430). Jōha quotes Sagoromo's greeting to the Princess, which mentions that the Crown Prince has asked to see these flowers at their peak. As with the Genji Princess, Jōha identifies this character at first mention. Also typical, he uses the character's final title in the tale. The Crown Prince's father reigns as the Ichijō Emperor.

28. See *SNKS* (1:10); *KCS* (430). Jōha quotes a description of the Genji Princess as more beautiful than the flowers Sagoromo gives her. The gloss has me stumped.

29. See *SNKS* (1:10) and *SNKZ* (1:18); *KCS* (430). *NKBT* (299–300) has *hana koso haru no*. I follow the formatting in the alternate version of *Undersash*; *SMKR* runs the heading and gloss together. Jōha quotes the Genji Princess's comment as she picks up the branch of kerria rose that Sagoromo and his page have just brought her. The gloss attempts to identify the allusion, suggesting that it comes from [*Collection of*] *Ten Thousand Leaves* (*Man'yō[shū]*, ca. 759). It then notes Teika's "words" (*kotoba*) and a verse from *Continued Collection of Ancient and Modern Japanese Poems* (Spring). *KCS* includes the particle *to* at the end of the heading, as if quoting the heading. *KCS* also lists an alternate ending to the poem (*tsuranekeri*, despite the presence of *koso* in line 4).

(10) cape jasmine dye cannot speak (*kuchi nashi ni shi mo* くちなしにしも):

山吹の花色衣ぬしやたれとへどこたへずくちなしにして

Who owns this garment	*yamabuki no*
bright yellow as the lovely	*hana irogoromo*
kerria roses?	*nushi ya tare*
I ask yet no reply comes:	*toedo kotaezu*
cape jasmine dye cannot speak.[30]	*kuchi nashi ni shi mo*

(11) like that (*saru wa* さるは):
This is Chūnagon's reply.[31]

(12) "what then should I do" poem (*ika ni sen no uta* いかにせんの哥):
This is a verse that the Major Captain recites to himself, comparing his feelings to kerria roses.[32]

(13) the twining columbine (*tatsu odamaki* たつをだまき):

谷ふかみたつをだまきは我なれやおもふ心の朽てやみぬる

In the valley's depths	*tani fukami*
the twining columbine climbs;	*tatsu odamaki wa*
surely, that is me!	*ware nare ya*
My heart that longs for her	*omou kokoro no*
will wind up rotting, in the end.	*kuchite yaminuru*

This poem is in book 3. [The allusion] means that no one knows [how Sagoromo feels].[33]

(14) "leaning on the main pillar" to "how painful!" (*moya no hashira ni yori kokorogurushiki ya made* もやのはしらにより心ぐるしきやまで):

---

30. See *SNKS* (1:10), *SNKZ* (1:18), and *NKBT* (30); *KCS* (430). Jōha quotes Sagoromo's own comment about the flowers, made as he silently burns for the Princess. The gloss identifies an allusion to *Collection of Ancient and Modern Japanese Poems* (Miscellaneous Forms, Sosei). I modify the translation from Rodd, *Kokinshū*, 349, using "kerria rose" for "wild mountain rose." This echoes the allusion to *Genji* noted earlier and clarifies the link to Sagoromo's related verse (gloss 12). Like that poem, the one noted here puns on the color of the flowers and the phrase "has no mouth."

31. See *SNKS* (1:10), *SNKZ* (1:18), and *NKBT* (30); *KCS* (430). Jōha quotes one of the Princess's attendants, introduced in gloss 5. The gloss notes her identity. She responds to Sagoromo's allusion in gloss 10.

32. See *SNKS* (1:10), *SNKZ* (1:18), and *NKBT* (30). Jōha quotes the first line of the poem; for a translation, see poem 1 in chapter 2 (*ika ni semu*) (he uses an alternate transcription of the last syllable). The gloss identifies this as verse as a *dokugin*, rather than one read aloud. It also notes the hero's iconic rank, but not the first one named in Jōha's copy of the tale or those consulted here. That is "middle captain" (*chūjō*), as seen in gloss 25.

33. See *SNKS* (1:10), *SNKZ* (1:18), and *NKBT* (30); *KCS* (430). Jōha quotes Sagoromo's thought after reciting the verse noted in gloss 12. The hero appears to allude to another poem. The gloss lists the first poem from book 3 of *Sagoromo*, presumably because the phrase in the heading serves as its second line. Other lines vary; see the extended note by the *NKBT* editors (217). On possible inspirations for the poem, see Gotō, "*Sagoromo monogatari* sakuchūka no haikei."

This must be the narrator's comment.[34]

(15) the Eight Islands of Muro (*Muro no Yashima* 室の八嶋):
The allusion is unclear. The meaning is obvious.[35]

(16) still, that smoke (*saru wa sono keburi* さるはそのけぶり):
This means that it is not that he cannot reveal his feelings, but that since they have been like siblings since they were twin leaves [he worries]. At that time, spouses were called "sister and brother."[36]

(17) the Minister, his mother, and the rest (*Otodo hahamiya nado mo* 大殿母宮なども):
It means that they would not think it should be this way.[37]

(18) [that had] start[ed] now (*ima hajime* いまはじめ):
From here on is the narrator's comment. It should end at "one should not treat [someone who is not a real brother] like that."[38]

(19) the dying wish of the late retired emperor (*koin no on'yuigon* 古院の御ゆいごん):
There are variants that have "early examples [include] the gentleman-in-waiting Nakazumi" and so on in this section.[39]

---

34. See *SNKS* (1:10), *SNKZ* (1:18), and *NKBT* (30); *KCS* (430). Jōha quotes from an extended description of the Genji Princess and of Sagoromo as he watches her; this passage also immediately follows the thought noted in gloss 13. The gloss credits the narrator with the closing judgment (*sōshi no ji naru beshi*). *KCS* includes the last word of the heading in the gloss.

35. See *SNKS* (1:10), *SNKZ* (1:18), and *NKBT* (30); *KCS* (430). Jōha quotes from Sagoromo's thought in the passage from gloss 14. These islands sit in the lake of a shrine in northern Japan. The mist rising from them evokes the smoke produced by hidden fires (i.e., secret passion). The series note a likely allusion. Jōha, too, suggests that the allusion is unknown. He adds that Sagoromo's feelings are readily intelligible (*kokoro wa kakure nashi*). *KCS* presents this gloss as Jōha's comment; unlike the version seen above, it does not appear in the smaller font that suggests supplementary material.

36. See *SNKS* (1:11), *SNKZ* (1:18), and *NKBT* (30); *KCS* (430). Jōha quotes from the narrator's comment on the allusion noted in gloss 15. The gloss essentially recapitulates the rest of the passage under discussion, including a reference to Sagoromo and the Genji Princess as seedlings. The last part of the gloss diverges sharply from the series. Those describe onlookers' view of the young people as siblings. Jōha observes that the word in question can mean man and wife.

37. See *SNKS* (1:11), *SNKZ* (1:20), and *NKBT* (31); *KCS* (430–31). While I have retained the standard format for legibility, there is no distinction between heading and gloss in either of my texts of *Undersash*. Judged from the series, Jōha skips ahead in Sagoromo's thoughts. His concern here is that people will not accept his love for the Princess. The gloss simply quotes his fear without commenting on it. The effect is to echo gloss 16, which suggests that Sagoromo imagines the problem. "Minister" or "Lord" (*otodo*) is a general term of respect for elite officials. Here it names Lord Horikawa, mentioned with his wife.

38. See *SNKS* (1:11) and *SNKZ* (1:20); *KCS* (431). *NKBT* (31) has *kyō*, not *ima*. Jōha again notes Sagoromo's passion for the Genji Princess. In the tale, the rest of the passage condemns Horikawa's decision to raise the children together. The gloss notes that this is the narrator's judgment and notes where the comment ends by giving the final suffix (*[motenasasetamōmajikari]kere*).

39. See *SNKS* (1:12), *SNKZ* (1:21), and *NKBT* (31); *KCS* (431). Jōha refers to the late emperor's instruction that the current emperor rely on Lord Horikawa to manage the government. The gloss quotes from a passage that compares Sagoromo to Nakazumi from *The Tale of Utsuho* (*Utsuho monogatari*, tenth century), who also falls in love with his full sister; see Uraki, *Tale of the Cavern*. These

(20) the younger sister of the late former emperor (*kosentei no imōto* 古
先帝のいもうと):
This is Sagoromo's mother.[40]

(21) Tōin (洞院):
The [daughter of the] Great Minister, the Go-Ichijō Retired
Emperor's grandfather.[41]

(22) Bōmon (坊門):
This is the daughter of the Princely Minister of Ceremonial, son of
a previous emperor.[42]

(23) the current emperor (*kinjō* 今上):
This is the Saga Retired Emperor's first son, the crown prince. He
is Lady Bōmon's grandson.[43]

(24) even in this company (*kakaru onnaka ni mo* かかる御中にも):
This recounts Sagoromo's birth to the Ise Priestess, after she
stepped down from her post and Lord Horikawa became her
guardian. From "even a son" is about Sagoromo.[44]

---

passages also invoke Kaoru from *Genji*, who harbors feelings for sisterlike characters. This passage precedes the phrase from the heading in *SNKZ* (1:20) and *NKBT*. *SNKS* does not contain it. The note in the gloss about variants (*ihon*) confirms that *Undersash* relies on a text similar to *SNKS*. It also supports Jōha's opening claim that he consulted various copies of the tale when compiling the commentary.

40. See *SNKS* (1:12), *SNKZ* (1:21), and *NKBT* (32); *KCS* (431). Jōha quotes from a passage introducing Lord Horikawa's "three main wives" (*sannin kita no kata*). The line at hand presents Lady Horikawa, already introduced in gloss 5. That comment uses an honorific to describe this character, as do all three versions of the tale noted here. The current heading does not, suggesting a variant in Jōha's copy of the tale. He resumes the use of honorifics for this character.

41. See *SNKS* (1:13), *SNKZ* (1:21), and *NKBT* (32); *KCS* (431). Jōha quotes from the same passage as gloss 20, introducing another of Lord Horikawa's wives. This woman, known as Lady Tōin, lives on the northeastern corner of the estate, bounded by the eponymous street and Nijō Ōji. The gloss is particularly interesting. Unlike the entries about Horikawa's other two wives, this one refers only to his father-in-law, stating the man's office and his relationship to the current Crown Prince; Lady Tōin's older sister is the current emperor's only named consort. By contrast, the versions of the tale used here identify Lady Tōin through her relationship to her sister and note that this makes Tōin the Crown Prince's aunt.

42. See *SNKS* (1:13), *SNKZ* (1:22), and *NKBT* (32); *KCS* (431). Jōha quotes from the description of Lord Horikawa's third wife, again naming her father. Since she lives in the southeast corner of the property, facing Sanjō Bōmon, the southern boundary of the estate, she is known as Lady Bōmon. The gloss follows my versions of the tale in identifying her through the Princely Minister of Ceremonial. Jōha may have added the detail about her grandfather; it does not appear in the series.

43. See *SNKS* (1:13), *SNKZ* (1:22), and *NKBT* (32); *KCS* (431). As in the two preceding entries, the heading is misleading; the gloss does not concern the character whose name comes first. The passage in question concerns the current emperor's son, born to Horikawa's only biological daughter. Jōha's emphasis on Lady Bōmon's relationship to the Prince is striking. Lord Horikawa's tie is the significant bond in terms of court politics; he will be grandfather to an emperor, but this tie goes unstressed.

44. See *SNKS* (1:13), *SNKZ* (1:22), and *NKBT* (32); *KCS* (431). Jōha quotes from the next passage in the tale, which formally introduces Sagoromo. The gloss stresses Lady Horikawa's special

(25) the Middle Captain of the Second Rank (*Nii no chūjō* 二位の中将):
This is Sagoromo's current office. It says that they do not make
him a counselor in deference to the Way of Heaven.[45]

(26) the sixteenth (*dai jūroku* 第十六):
Three thousand dust-particle kalpas in the past, there was a buddha
called the Buddha Great Universal Wisdom Excellence. When this
Buddha was still a prince, he had sixteen children. After he achieved
enlightenment, they went to the place where he was and became
his disciples. When he entered nirvana, these sixteen bodhisattvas
became buddhas in the ten directions for the benefit of all living
things. The sixteenth prince preached enlightenment in this world
of suffering. In other words, he is today's Sakyamuni.[46]

(27) big enough to cover up (*ōu bakari no* おほふばかりの):

大空におほふばかりの袖もがな春ちる花を風にまかせじ

I wish I had sleeves	*ōzora ni*
big enough to cover up	*ōu bakari no*
the entire sky.	*sode mogana*
I would not leave to the wind	*haru chiru hana o*
the blossoms that fall in spring.[47]	*kaze ni makaseji*

---

background, her husband's regard for her, and their initial familial relationship. The remark about the
hero is equally striking. Elite courtiers favored daughters, used for political marriages.

45. See *SNKS* (1:14), *SNKZ* (1:22), and *NKBT* (32); *KCS* (431). In the series, the heading skips past
a description of Lord and Lady Horikawa's great love for Sagoromo to identify the hero's current
office, granted at the age of "seventeen or eighteen" by the old Japanese count; *SNKS* suggests the
latter. The narrator in the series notes that this is a typical appointment for elite youths; giving them
higher posts would tempt fate. Jōha presents a more distinctive explanation for Sagoromo's case, cit-
ing "the Way of Heaven" (*Tentō*). This term also appears in the history noted earlier; see Brown and
Ishida, *The Future and the Past*, 453.

46. See *SNKS* (1:14), *SNKZ* (1:23), and *NKBT* (33); *KCS* (431). I follow the *SMKR* editor in correct-
ing "ten ten-thousands" (*jūman*) to "the ten directions" (*jippō*). Jōha quotes from the next passage in
the tale, which returns to Sagoromo's parents. They think of the hero as their own incarnation of
the historical Buddha, known in Japan as Shaka Nyorai. In the seventh chapter of the Lotus Sutra,
known as the "Parable of the Phantom City," the Buddha describes himself as the sixteenth son of
Great Universal Wisdom Excellence (*Daitsūchishō-butsu*); see Watson, *Lotus Sutra*, 117–34. The gloss
retells that story, probably from the sutra; none of the versions of *Sagoromo* consulted goes into much
detail. A dust-particle kalpa (*jintengō*) is the immense span of time during which a buddha visits all
the worlds in one of the ten directions. *KCS* specifies thirty kalpas, not three thousand.

47. *SNKS* (1:14) only; *KCS* (431). I follow the *SMKR* editor in correcting *omou* to *ōu*, seen in *KCS*.
Jōha quotes from later in the same passage of the tale, still centered on Sagoromo's parents. Here
they wish to protect their son from the world. The gloss notes their allusion to an anonymous verse
from *Later Collection of Japanese Poems*.

(28) Considering this world ephemeral (*kono yo o ba karisome ni oboshimeshite* 此世をばかりそめにおぼしめして):
This means that, since [Sagoromo] wishes to seek the Buddhist path, he does not set his heart on anyone. In the book it says that, as a result, ordinary persons find him aloof.[48]

(29) pleasantries (*kagoto* かごと):
These are merely superficial.[49]

(30) *(Make those autumn nights)* a round thousand, all one night (*chiyo o hitoyo ni* 千夜を一夜に):

秋の夜の千代を一夜になせりとも詞のこりて鳥や鳴なん

Make those autumn nights,	*aki no yo no*
a round thousand, all one night,	*chiyo o hito yo ni*
and when it was done,	*naseri to mo*
we would still be whispering	*kotoba nokorite*
while the rooster crowed at dawn.	*tori ya nakinan*

[The allusion] is just words.[50]

(31) *(Is it then because she is grass upon)* the reefs that drown in the tide (*irinu iso no* 入ぬるいその):

---

48. See *KCS* (431) only. I follow the latter version in separating the heading from the gloss. None of the series gives the line in the heading as written. *SNKS* (1:15) is the closest. *SNKZ* (1:23) and *NKBT* (34) add a quotation from the eighteenth chapter of the Lotus Sutra, titled "The Benefits of Responding with Joy" (see Watson, *Lotus Sutra*, 245–50). Jōha presumably leaves Sagoromo's parents to quote from a passage about the hero. The gloss elaborates on his feelings and how people respond to him (the series' editors specify women). The word translated as book is *sōshi*.

49. See *SNKS* (1:16) only; *KCS* (431). In *SNKS*, Jōha quotes from a description of Sagoromo's correspondence. I follow the *SMKR* editor in correcting *oto* to *soto*, seen in *KCS*. However, *oto* might work, since the hero silences his true feelings. The gloss notes that he takes no pleasure in such things, also the view of the *SNKS* editor.

50. *SNKS* (1:16), *SNKZ* (1:25), and *NKBT* (34); *KCS* (431). I have formatted this entry myself. It lingers on Sagoromo's female correspondent, identifying a related allusion to a poem in episode 22 of *Tales of Ise*. My translation, adapted from Mostow and Tyler (*Ise Stories*, 63), separates the allusion from the rest of the verse. *SMKR* uses the last four lines of the verse as its heading; the poem's first line precedes this as an interlinear note, crowned with a virgule. *KCS* mystifyingly prefaces the entire gloss with a partial allusion from the same passage. The comment at the end of all this poetry observes that Senji borrows words, rather than a theme; this recalls gloss 2. Technically, *SMKR* uses the Chinese character for "a thousand ages," not "a thousand nights," but the series agree with *Ise*. *KCS*, which uses phonetic characters, is ambiguous.

塩みてば入ぬる磯の草なれやみらくすくなくこふらくのおほき

Is it then because	*shio miteba*
she is grass upon the reefs	*irinuru iso no*
that drown in the tide?	*kusa nareya*
Few are the times I see her,	*miraku sukunaku*
many the hours of longing.[51]	*kouraku no ōki*

(32) Inabuchi (*Inabuchi* いなぶち):

年をふる涙はいかに逢事はなをいなぶちの瀧まされとや

Along with the years	*toshi o furu*
my tears stream down, and still we	*namida wa ika ni*
never seem to meet;	*au koto wa*
must Inabuchi Falls, then,	*nao Inabuchi no*
spill still more water from their depths?	*taki masare to ya*

This is a famous place in Yamato. [The allusion] means that Sagoromo wears himself out with longing.[52]

(33) found the fields so fair (*no o natsukashimi* 野をなつかしみ):

---

51. See *SNKS* (1:16), *SNKZ* (1:25), and *NKBT* (34). I again format the entry myself. *SMKR* lists the last four lines of the poem, again preceded by the first line and virgule as interlinear notes. I follow the *SMKR* editor in ignoring the duplicate *kusa no*; this text, unlike *KCS*, lists it twice. *KCS* lists the entire verse. This gloss concerns the same passage and subject as the previous two: women enamored of the hero. In order to reproduce that effect, I quote two lines from Cranston, *Grasses of Remembrance*, 663. The allusion is likely to *Collection of Gleanings of Japanese Poems* (Love). *KCS* gives the first line as *shio meteba*.

52. See *SNKS* (1:16), *SNKZ* (1:25), and *NKBT* (34); *KCS* (431–32). Jōha quotes from the end of the passage that has occupied Jōha since gloss 29. The first half of the gloss identifies another allusion, to a poem included in *Continued Collection of Ancient and Modern Japanese Poems* (Love, Minamoto Tomouji). In *KCS*, this poem closes with the particle *ka*. The attribution is unlikely unless a medieval copyist added the poem to the tale; Tomouji died in 1287. None of the series presents the poem in this form; even *KCS* ends differently, with *namida ka*. *NKBT* suggests an earlier verse. The second half of the gloss explains the allusion, noting that Inabuchi is a *meisho* or famous place. Poets exploit its "deep pools" (*fuchi*) to describe emotions that come out in tears (the falls). Jōha ends by suggesting that the line refers to Sagoromo, pining for the Genji Princess. The series' editors instead point to his correspondents, who weep over his casual visits. *KCS* agrees: this text contains an additional line saying "This must be how the persons with whom Sagoromo occasion-ally corresponds feel." *SMKR* and *KCS* cite variants of the poem by Tomouji; in the second line, *SMKR* has *namida wa*; *KCS* has *namida ka*. Both versions of *Undersash* refer to the hero. The prefix appears in phonetic script.

春の野にすみれつみにとこし我ぞ野をなつかしみ一夜ねにける

I came to spring fields   *haru no no ni*
to pick violets, but   *sumire tsumi ni to*
found the fields so fair   *koshi ware zo*
that I spent the whole night there,   *no o natsukashimi*
sleeping among the flowers.[53]   *hitoyo nenikeru*

(34) the Brahma's Net Sutra (*Bonmōkyō* 梵網経):
This is the concluding sutra of the Flower Garland Sutra. (*There may be a mistake in the original. One should compare [texts].*) With one glance at a woman, one often loses the virtue of his eyes. (*This is a line in the Flower Garland Sutra.*) This is not in the Brahma's Net Sutra. What the author identifies as the concluding sutra is the second chapter that we read today. Again, when I asked, [I was told that] it is in the first chapter.[54]

(35) (*At the Nison-in on the twenty-ninth day of the intercalary First [Month]*) even that (*sa dani wa* さだには):
It means how could that line from the sutra [be correct].[55]

(36) the koto (*koto wa* 琴は):
Unseasonal frost and snow fall. It says that unless these skills are passed on, there will be divine punishment.[56]

---

53. See *SNKS* (1:16), *SNKZ* (1:25), and *NKBT* (35); *KCS* (432). Jōha quotes from a passage hinting at Sagoromo's trysts. The gloss identifies a poem that appears in several collections, notably the preface to *Collection of Ancient and Modern Japanese Poems* (the poet is Akahito; see Rodd, *Kokinshū*, 42–43). I retranslate it to foreground the allusion. *SNKZ* and *NKBT* also allude to the poem earlier in this passage, with the phrase *sumire tsumi ni wa.*

54. See *SNKS* (1:16), *SNKZ* (1:25), and *NKBT* (35); *KCS* (432). Jōha quotes from the same passage discussed in gloss 33. Here the hero recalls a line from a sutra, which he tentatively attributes to the text named above. The gloss identifies that text, then questions the accuracy of this ascription. While the line does not appear in the Brahma's Net Sutra as we know it, Nichiren (1222–82) also stressed this teaching, which he ties to the Flower Garland Sutra; see Ueki, *Gender Equality in Buddhism*, 4, cited in Paludi and Ellens, *Feminism and Religion*, 120. *KCS* includes the material from gloss 35 in the middle of this entry, between *"(This is a line in the Flower Garland Sutra.)"* and *"This is not in the Brahma's Net Sutra."*

55. See *SNKS* (1:17), *SNKZ* (1:26), and *NKBT* (35); heading not given in *KCS*. Jōha quotes from the final part of the passage discussed in the previous two entries, at least as seen in the series. There the narrator suggests that even the otherworldly Sagoromo takes an interest in women. Jōha paraphrases this comment, suggesting that the warning about women should not apply in this case. The interlinear note—marked with a virgule and presumably misplaced—gives the date and location of Jōha's search for the sutra. Nison-in venerates two buddhas, Shaka and Amida. Jōha had family and poetic ties there, as did the Sanjōnishi.

56. See—very approximately—*SNKS* (1:17), *SNKZ* (1:26), and *NKBT* (35); *KCS* (432). Jōha apparently quotes from a passage discussing Sagoromo's musical talents. The gloss highlights their unearthly effects and suggests that the gods wish him to pass on this gift. None of the series mentions

(37) Amewakamiko (あめわかみこ):
He descended to earth. This appears in the first part of the second book of *Nihongi*. Amewakahiko.[57]

(38) the Genji Princess (*Genji no miya* 源氏宮):
The previous emperor [was] Retired Emperor Enyū. [She is his] imperial princess. *Her mother was Chūnagon no Suke. She [the princess] is Sagoromo's cousin.* She is the niece of Sagoromo's mother *(originally the Ise Priestess).*[58]

(39) just like the (Sagoromo) Middle Captain (*Chūjō to onaji gotoku ni* 中将と同じごとくに):
[Lord and Lady Horikawa] raised [the Genji Princess] just like the Middle Captain.[59]

(40) Itada (*Itada no* いただの):
[Collection of] Ten Thousand Leaves:

the second point and only two note anything like the results mentioned initially. Instead, after asserting the hero's good looks and intelligence, these copies mention his talents on the flute and koto; *SNKS* and *NKBT* note that his music "moves heaven and earth" (*ametsuchi o [mo] ugokashi*). *NKBT* also says that his playing "unsettles people's hearts" (*hito no kokoro o odorokashi*). All of these properties recall early discussions of *waka*. *KCS* does not separate the heading and gloss.

57. See *SNKS* (1:18) only; *KCS* (432). *SMKR* includes an untranslated interlinear gloss that gives the phonetic pronunciation of the name at the end of the entry; the name itself is written in Chinese characters. Jōha names the god of music featured in Sanetaka's play (chapter 4). The god's name is given in phonetic script. This passage does not describe the miracle associated with this figure, which Senji relates later. Reflecting on Sagoromo's musical talents, his parents wonder if he might not be the god come to earth. They also worry that another being of this kind will bring a heavenly robe and take their son to the heavens. In the tale, this actually happens. Jōha gives a precedent for such miracles and an alternate name for the god. *SNKZ* (1:26) mentions "heavenly beings" (*tennin*) but recalls *NKBT* above; Sagoromo's music "unsettles" even them.

58. See *SNKS* (1:18), *SNKZ* (1:27), and *NKBT* (36). *SMKR* marks the entry with a virgule. Jōha quotes from the formal introduction to the Genji Princess. He adds two details, at least compared to the series. First, he identifies another connection to Emperor Enyū, described earlier in *Undersash* as Lord Horikawa's father. Second, he identifies the Princess's mother with the label *suke* (nominally second in command in various settings) rather than *miyasudokoro*, seen in the series. The second label signals that she gave birth to an emperor's child. Jōha seems to suggest that she held a lower rank.

59. See—approximately—*SNKS* (1:18), *SNKZ* (1:28), and *NKBT* (36); *KCS* (432). *SMKR* presents the material in one line; I have added the heading by recycling the first phrase, which is why the gloss seems redundant. None of the series contains this phrase. *KCS* (which gives the content in *SMKR* as its gloss) also has something different. Jōha discusses how Sagoromo's parents raised the Genji Princess as his sister. *KCS*'s heading (*chūjō no onajigoto ni*) means the same thing as that given above. The series vary but share *onaji kokoro*, "the same feelings." There is another heading between this gloss and the next one in *KCS*, but no gloss.

をはただのいただのはしのこぼれなばけたよりゆかんこふ
なわぎもこ

In Owatada,	Owatada no
if the bridge at Itada	Itada no hashi no
should fall to ruin,	koborenaba
I would use the beams to go	keta yori yukan
to you, beloved, never fear.	kouna wagimoko

This does not mean the Genji Princess; [Sagoromo] peeks to see if anyone resembles her.[60]

(41) Silent (*Oto nashi no* をとなしの):

こひ侘てひとりふせやによもすがらおつるなみだやをとな
しのたき

Miserable with love,	koiwabite
alone in my wretched hut	hitori fuseya ni
all throughout the night,	yomosugara
the tears spilling down my cheeks	otsuru namida ya
are the Silent Waterfall.	Oto nashi no taki

(*A poem by Kiyowara Motosuke*):

をとなしの河とぞつゐにながれ出るいはでものおもふ人の
なみだは

So, then, it is as	Oto nashi no
the Silent River that they	kawa to zo tsui ni
come welling out,	nagareizuru
the tears of someone	iwade mono omou
who loves without speaking his heart.	hito no namida wa

This poem fits. Alternatively:

---

60. See *SNKS* (1:19) only; *KCS* (432). Jōha quotes a single word from a description of Sagoromo contrasting his steadfast passion for the Genji Princess with the nocturnal wanderings of the hero of the lost Heian tale *The Cloak of Invisibility* (*Kakuremino*); he apparently used his coat to spy on women. The gloss, marked by a virgule, identifies the poem, supplemented by the name of the collection. Jōha clarifies that Sagoromo is not involved with the Princess; he merely pursues other women who might resemble her. As the *SNKS* editor notes, *Collection of Ten Thousand Leaves* locates the bridge in Owarida, not Owatada.

いかにしていかによからんをの山の上よりおつる音なしのたき

What am I to do,	*ika ni shite*
and how would I be better off?	*ika ni yokaran*
On Mount Ono	*Onoyama no*
it flows from the very peak,	*ue yori otsuru*
the Silent Waterfall.	*Oto nashi no taki*

This [waterfall is in] Jōshū.[61]

(42) Shinobu pattern (*Shinobu mojizuri* しのぶもぢずり):
He is not just upset; he must have hidden feelings.[62]

(43) the Great Minister (*Ōki otodo* 大おとど):
The daughter of the Great Minister takes in Ima Himegimi and
tries to [marry] her to the Go-Ichijō Retired Emperor. Lady Dōin
[is] Lord Horikawa's main wife.[63]

(44) the Crown Prince (*Tōgū* 春宮):
The Go-Ichijō Retired Emperor. The [character] identified as the
emperor is the Ichijō Retired Emperor.[64]

---

61. See *SNKS* (1:19) only; *KCS* (432). *NKBT* 37 has *Yoshino no taki*. Jōha quotes from the same passage as before. Now the focus is on Sagoromo's frustration, which expresses itself in tears. Since the phrase quoted appears in numerous poems, Jōha considers possible allusions. It lists a verse in *Collection of Verbal Flowers* (*Shikashū*, 1151) (Love, Fujiwara Toshitada); another in *Collection of Gleanings of Japanese Poems* (Love, Kiyowara Motosuke); and a third from a commentary on *Genji's* "Evening Mist" (*Yūgiri*) chapter; for an alternate translation off that poem, see Tyler, *Tale of Genji*, 740 n. 59. The first verse is marked with a virgule, while the second follows a triangle. There is another virgule beside the word *namida*; this is also the location of the character translated as "verify" (*tadasu*) above. *KCS* specifies that the first waterfall is in Kishū and that the verse draws on Motosuke's poem; this is presumably the meaning of the triangle in *SMKR*. After the third verse, *KCS* repeats that the waterfall is in Kishū.

62. See *SNKS* (1:19), *SNKZ* (1:29), and *NKBT* (37); *KCS* (432). Jōha presents another poetic phrase referencing Sagoromo's love for the Genji Princess. The phrase in the heading evokes *Tales of Ise*: more precisely, a poem in the first episode, in which the hero flirts with two sisters in a witty verse about his wild passion (*midare*) by sending them a strip of a robe printed in *shinobu* or fern-print pattern; for a translation, see Mostow and Tyler, *Ise Stories*, 5. The name of the design puns on secret longing. In the series, the editors state that Senji emphasizes secrecy. Jōha makes the same point. The *SNKZ* editors note that *midare* (like the allusion to *Ise*) recurs throughout this subplot. Jōha minimizes this thread throughout *Undersash*, presumably for its subversive implications. The hero of *Ise* is known for his political ambitions, expressed by seducing imperial women. Senji also suggests this; see the introduction.

63. See *SNKS* (1:20), *SNKZ* (1:29), and *NKBT* (37); *KCS* (432). Jōha quotes from a passage about Lord Horikawa's wife Tōin, introduced in gloss 21. It concerns Tōin's desire for a child of her own; she is the only of Lord Horikawa's wives without one. Jōha clarifies the reference to Tōin and identifies the young woman whom she adopts and Tōin's larger ambitions; see D'Etcheverry, *Love after "The Tale of Genji,"* 72–79, on this subplot. The Retired Go-Ichijō Emperor is currently the Crown Prince.

64. See *SNKS* (1:20), *SNKZ* (1:29), and *NKBT* (37); *KCS* (432–33). Jōha quotes from a description of the Crown Prince's desire for the Genji Princess. The gloss identifies the Prince's final office, as

(45) on the Middle Captain's way home from the palace (*Chūjō uchi yori idetamō michi ni* 中将内より出で給ふ道に):
It says that there are no peasants without sweet flags dangling from their arms.[65]

(46) the village of Tōchi (*Tōchi no sato* 十市の里):
Allusion unknown. This appears in *His Majesty's Yakumo Treatise*. It only means distant. "There is no other meaning for Tōchi."[66]

(47) their faces and so on, too (*kao nado mo* かほなども):
It says that they are carrying so many sweet flags that one cannot see their faces. He reproves his escort for stopping them and making them wait at attention.[67]

(48) since they're used to it (*narai ni te saburaeba* ならひにて さぶらへば):
This is the escorts' response.[68]

(49) the path of love (*koi no michi o ba* こひのみちをば):
[It] is filled with painful experience—these are the Major Captain's words, as he thinks of himself.[69]

---

before, and clarifies a reference to his father. *KCS* (432) begins the comment with the particle *wa*, turning the entire entry into a sentence.

65. See *SNKS* (1:20), *SNKZ* (1:30), and *NKBT* (38); all three more closely resemble *KCS* (433): *Chūjō no kimi uchi yori makan idetamō michi ni*. Jōha quotes from a passage set on the fourth day of the Fifth Month. This is the eve of the Sweet Flag Festival (*Tango no sekku*), when nobles decorated their homes and hair with sweet flags (*shōbu*). Jōha notes the vendors whom Sagoromo sees thronging the street. "Peasants" translates *shizu no o*.

66. See *SNKS* (1:21), *SNKZ* (1:30), and *NKBT* (38); *KCS* (433). There is a virgule at the start of the gloss. Jōha refers to Sagoromo's thoughts as he looks out from his carriage on the scene just noted. In the series, he actually thinks of "Tōchi's muddy path" (*Tōchi no koiji*, the second word punning on "paths of love"; see chapter 3 (n. 3). Jōha admits that he cannot identify the allusion. Then he quotes *Yakumo mishō* (1234), by Emperor Juntoku (r. 1210–21), to explain the pun on the village's name. I am not sure how to attribute the final remarks. *SMKR* gives the last sentence in phonetic transcription (*katakana*); *KCS* has the more typical mixture of Chinese characters and another syllabary (*hiragana*). It also presents the whole gloss as a supplementary comment.

67. See *SNKS* (1:21), *SNKZ* (1:30), and *NKBT* (38); *KCS* (433). Jōha returns to the peddlers. In the series, the narrator has already pointed out that their legs are covered in dirt. Jōha notes Sagoromo's command that his men stop harassing them while clearing the street for his carriage; the peddlers are burdened (and dirty) enough without having to crouch respectfully as he passes. *KCS* has a longer heading, extended through the first phrase of the gloss. Neither version of *Undersash* mentions the poem about the plants' roots given in the notes to "Sagoromo's Sleeves" in chapter 3 (*ukishizumi*).

68. See *SNKS* (1:21), *SNKZ* (1:31), and *NKBT* (38); *KCS* (433). Jōha quotes the hero's retainers, who insist that the peddlers can bear up under their loads and (implicitly) the rough treatment. The gloss simply clarifies who is speaking.

69. See *SNKS* (1:21) and—approximately—*SNKZ* (1:31) and *NKBT* (38); *KCS* (433). *SMKR* presents the material in one line. I follow *KCS* in separating the quotation from the gloss. None of the series

(50) fan as flute (*ōgi o fue* 扇 を 笛):
Blowing across the fan is a common behavior. *Skin flute* appears in
Genji. It means whistling.[70]

(51) *hajitomi* (*hashitomi* は し と み):
Half-shutters. *Genji*. This resembles the "Evening Faces"
chapter.[71]

(52) like them (*are ga* あ れ が):
This is how the attendants feel as they watch the Major Captain's
carriage pass, wishing they could just be in his escort.[72]

(53) an iris from the eaves (*noki no ayame o* 軒のあやめを):
They pull it down and chase down the stragglers in his escort to
present it.[73]

(54) Shiranuma (*Shiranuma no* し ら ぬ ま の):
Perhaps "white marsh." It may pun on the phrase "while not
knowing." "White Marsh" has not been identified. Perhaps it
means "white waves," or the like. The poem is obvious.[74]

---

has the phrase quoted in the heading, although *SNKS* comes very close with the synonym *koiji*. This is the same phrase that apparently does not appear in the earlier section of Jōha's text. *SNKZ* and *NKBT* have *koi no mochibu*, "porter of love." All three series contemplate Sagoromo's response to his men's remarks; since he feels a kinship with the peddlers, due to his own suffering, he finds his escort lacking in sympathy. As in the previous comment, Jōha simply identifies who is speaking. *KCS* specifies that this is internal monologue (*shinshi* or *kokoro no kotoba*). Both versions of *Undersash* return to naming the hero by his iconic rank.

70. See *SNKS* (1:22) only; *KCS* (433). We remain in the passage under review since gloss 45. In *SNKS*, Sagoromo looks pityingly at the poor houses and blows across his fan as if it were a flute; the editor sees this as showing the hero at his ease, part of his "shining" (*hikaru*) beauty at sunset. *SNKZ* (1:31) and *NKBT* (38) share that detail. *NKBT* comes closer to *SNKS*: the hero plays a (real) flute and like *SNKS* describes the poor houses as grass huts. The gloss explains the phrase and notes a precedent. "Skin flute" (*kawabue*) presumably refers to the lips. *KCS* specifies *kababue*, which it includes in the regular gloss.

71. See *SNKS* (1:23), *SNKZ* (1:31), and *NKBT* (38); *KCS* (433). Jōha pivots to the persons watching Sagoromo from inside the poor houses. The gloss identifies the word in question by rewriting it in Chinese characters, then noting the echo of *Genji*. Instead of *omokage*, Jōha mentions a resemblance (*nitari*). The second term appears to describe a more limited allusion.

72. See *SNKS* (1:22), *SNKZ* (1:31), and *NKBT* (39); *KCS* (433). *SMKR* includes two small circles set off to the left immediately after the heading. Jōha quotes the thoughts of the people behind the shutters as they watch Sagoromo and his retinue pass. The gloss details their feelings and identifies them as a group.

73. See *SNKS* (1:22), *SNKZ* (1:31), and *NKBT* (39); *KCS* (433). Jōha redirects our attention to the women's actions: in the series, some younger members of the household pull a flower—now labeled *ayame*—from the eaves and send it to him with a poem. This alternate label for the plant previously called *shōbu* enables a pun on "pattern" or "distinction." The gloss explains how they get this plant to the hero. The heading in *KCS* specifies "one stalk" (*hito suji*) of iris.

74. See *SNKS* (1:22), *SNKZ* (1:32), and *NKBT* (39); *KCS* (433). Jōha quotes the first line of the women's poem, given in phonetic script; *KCS* adds the Chinese character for "poem" at the end of it. For a translation of the verse in question, see poem 2 in chapter 2 (*shiranuma no*). The gloss considers different meanings of the phrase, written in varying Chinese characters. Jōha concludes that the

(55) quick-witted (*kokoro toki* 心とき):
      A clever retainer sets out an inkstone.[75]

(56) folded paper (*tatangami* たたん紙):
      This word also appears in *Genji*. *Genji* does not contain *katakana*; it
      is [all] grass script. They say that this is commonly called Yamato
      kana.[76]

(57) "without noticing" poem (*mi mo wakade no uta* 見もわかでの哥):
      It says that there are too many irises thatching the eaves to see.[77]

(58) he didn't even consider casual affairs and the like, only forbidden
      [ones] (*uchitsukesō nado wa waza to onkokoro ni irazu tada
      arumajiki* うちつけけさうなどはわざと御心にいらずただ
      あるまじき):
      He is inexorably drawn to the Genji Princess, the Cloistered
      Princess, and others.[78]

---

poem itself is clear: *kakure nashi* (literally, there are no hidden spots). "'White waves,' or the like"
corrects *SMKR*'s *shiranami nami* to *shiranami nado*, seen in *KCS*.

75. See *SNKS* (1:23) only; *KCS* (433). Jōha quotes an approving description of one of Sagoromo's
retainers, who responds instantly to the delivery of the poem just noted. The gloss explains the com-
pliment. *SNKZ* (1:32) and *NKBT* (39) simply note that the escort—whether as a group (*mizuijindomo*)
or an individual (*mizuijin*)—finds the hero a brush.

76. See *SNKS* (1:23), *SNKZ* (1:32), and *NKBT* (39); *KCS* (433). Jōha notes the medium on which
Sagoromo writes his response to the verse noted earlier, the standard folded sheets that noblemen
carried with them for occasions like this. *SNKZ* and *NKBT* describe this particular piece of paper as
speckled with gold and silver, and probably intended for copying sutras; conveniently, these decora-
tions also evoke the mud clinging to the sweet flag/iris roots. In my note to gloss 46, I observed that
Jōha's text does not seem to include references to "love's muddy path." This gloss provides further
support for that claim. Jōha also makes another point. Instead of noting the beautiful paper, he
observes that *tatangami* also appears in *Genji* and that Sagoromo's disguised handwriting—using the
formal phonetic syllabary noted earlier—is uncommon in this context. Since it is very common in
writing by priests, the original passage in the tale likely mentioned sutra-paper and the formal script.
The references to "grass" and "Yamato *kana*" evoke the informal syllabary noted above, *hiragana*.
KCS ends with different phrase (*iu nari* rather than the *unun*).

77. See *SNKS* (1:23) and *SNKZ* (1:32); *KCS* (433). Jōha quotes the first line of Sagoromo's reply to
the verse noted in gloss 54. The present comment explains the poem as Sagoromo's excuse for not
visiting his correspondent. It is difficult to know what Jōha's copy of the poem looked like. *NKBT*
(39) has *mi mo wakazu* in the first line and *SNKZ* differs from *SNKS* in the fourth. In *SNKS*, the full
verse reads as follows: "Without knowing it, / I seem to have passed you by, / but in my defense, /
there is not a glimpse of eave / anywhere, just irises" (*mi mo wakade suginikeru ka na oshinabete noki
no ayame no hima shi nakereba*).

78. See *SNKS* (1:23), *SNKZ* (1:33), and *NKBT* (39); *KCS* (433). Jōha quotes a line shortly after the
incident with the irises, at least in the series. This passage seems stable across texts: *SNKS* and *SNKZ*
are almost identical, and *NKBT*'s different phrasing makes the same point. The gloss specifies "for-
bidden" relationships. Interestingly, while the editors of the series only note the Genji Princess here,
Jōha adds the Second Princess (named by her final title, after she takes vows) "and others." The last
part is shrewd. The tale's other major heroine—Asukai—is exactly the kind of lover that Sagoromo
supposedly avoids: someone beneath his rank.

(59) the paper's skin (*kami no hadae* 紙のはだへ):
It is good [quality]. This is an unusual expression.[79]

(60) his poems (*on'utadomo* 御哥ども):
This is the author of the book being humble.[80]

(61) the Consort from the Major Captain of the Left (*Sadaishō no nyōgo* 左大将の女御):
[She serves] the Go-Ichijō Retired Emperor, currently the crown prince. She has met Sagoromo in secret. He writes in his verse, "today, among irises."[81]

(62) "longing all this time" poem (*koiwataru uta* こひわたる哥):
It says that, on the fifth, one "cries" out, punning on cutting "roots."[82]

(63) the daughter of the Ichijō Retired Emperor (*Ichijō'in no himemiya* 一条院の姫宮):
In book 3 she marries Sagoromo. In book 4 she dies.[83]

(64) Because he could not see her clearly (ほのかなりしかば):
It says that he couldn't see well and thus couldn't judge. "In the letter to Shōshō" is a likeness of "in the letter to Shōnagon" in *Genji*'s "Young Murasaki."[84]

---

79. See *SNKS* (1:23) only; *KCS* (433). Jōha quotes from a description of the paper on which the hero sends out social notes the next day for the Sweet Flag Festival. The gloss tries to explain the word but says that it is rare. This may be due to an error in transcription; *KCS* gives *irohadae* ("colored skin") as the heading, with the entire preceding comment presented as gloss. *SNKS* is very close, using the term just noted. *SNKZ* (1:33) and *NKBT* (40) refer to the paper's color and underdrawings.

80. See *SNKS* (1:23), *SNKZ* (1:33), and *NKBT* (40); *KCS* (433). Jōha references the poems that Sagoromo sends on the paper discussed in the previous comment. While the wording differs (*SNKZ* and *NKBT* are close), the series say that Sagoromo's efforts are poor even by ordinary standards, and that the narrator must have gotten them wrong.

81. See *SNKS* (1:24), *SNKZ* (1:34), and *NKBT* (40); *KCS* (433). Jōha finally names Sagoromo's correspondent of the previous night, whom the tale identifies as the Sen'yōden Consort. The gloss identifies her husband, confirms her dalliance with the hero, and quotes from his verse to her in one of the letters discussed; for a translation of the poem, see the notes to the play in chapter 4 (*koiwataru*).

82. See *SNKS* (1:24), *SNKZ* (1:34), and *NKBT* (40); *KCS* (433). Jōha quotes the first line of the verse just noted. He explains the poem's central pun, inspired by the woman's gift on the day of the festival. There is an interlinear correction (*tatsu* for *satsu*) by the phrase "cutting [roots]." *KCS* has a different gloss: "On the fifth, at least, crying [*ne sae*], punning on 'root,' [is permissible]." This comment seems to reflect a different poem; the series have a slightly different verse. *SNKS* is closer to *KCS*.

83. See *SNKS* (1:24), *SNKZ* (1:34), and *NKBT* (40); *KCS* (434). Jōha moves on to a new character, the Ippon Princess (see the introduction). In the series, the heading immediately follows the poem just discussed. Here Sagoromo recalls a glimpse of the current emperor's eldest daughter—better known by the title just given—and wishes that he could see more. Jōha notes that Sagoromo eventually marries her, but not that he does so against his will. The broader comment appears to have been written later, as a supplementary note; the second one appears in the gloss itself. *KCS* gives both locations in the gloss.

84. See *SNKS* (1:24), *SNKZ* (1:34), and *NKBT* (40); *KCS* (434). I follow the *SMKR* editor's suggestion that "young princess" (*waka miya*) be read as *wakamurasaki*, the chapter title in *Genji*. *KCS* has this from the beginning, in phonetic script. Jōha quotes from the same passage, which considers the

(65) "while thinking of you" poem (*omoitsutsu uta* お も ひ つ つ 哥):
There is no difference.[85]

(66) the same (*onaji* お な じ):
It says that the writer abbreviates [the rest].[86]

(67) until they grew dark with cloves (*chōji ni kuromu made zo* 丁子にく
ろむまでぞ):
"Sprinkled" must mean that they are dyed.[87]

(68) on Mount Otowa and so on (*Otowa no yama ni wa nado* をとはの
山にはなど):
There must be an allusion.[88]

(69) "sinking into grief alone" poem (*uki ni nomi shizumu uta* うきにの
みしづむ哥):
It says that a sinking body does not readily float with tears. Grief
must [also] mean mire.[89]

---

reason for Sagoromo's interest in the Princess. The gloss paraphrases this section, then identifies a
model for his peeping. Shōshō and Shōnagon are the attendants of the Ippon Princess and Mura-
saki, respectively. *KCS* treats the second half of the gloss, about the allusion to *Genji*, as a separate
comment.

85. See *SNKS* (1:24), *SNKZ* (1:34), and *NKBT* (40); *KCS* (434). For a translation of this poem, see
poem 3 in chapter 2 (*omoitsutsu*); as noted there, *NKBT* gives a different last line. Sagoromo sends it
to the Ippon Princess through her attendant. The gloss (in the original, *kotonaru koto nashi*) equates
Sagoromo's verse—again, for a woman he does not want to marry—with Genji's first verse to the
love of his life, whom he shortly adopts. This remarkable claim privileges the poems' content over
their narrative context.

86. See *SNKS* (1:24), *SNKZ* (1:35), and *NKBT* 40; *KCS* (434). Jōha quotes from a description of
Sagoromo's other letters on the day of the festival, apparently just like this one. The gloss restates the
narrator's explanation for not discussing more of them, but attributes that statement to the author
or copyist (*hissha*). The use of the verb "to abbreviate" (*morasu*) recalls the homophone used at the
beginning of "Sagoromo's Sleeves," "to leak"; see chapter 3. The series all use another double-edged
verb in the passage at hand: *todomu*, "to stop [writing]" and "to record." *SNKS* diverges from the other
two texts in the rest of the section.

87. See *SNKS* (1:25), *SNKZ* (1:35), and, more distant, *NKBT* (40); *KCS* (434). Jōha leaves Sago-
romo's correspondence to consider his clothing. In the series, the hero wears dark, fragrant robes
(known as *chōji-zome*) and scarlet trousers. The gloss clarifies the verb used to describe the dyeing
process. *KCS* formats the entry differently, including up through "sprinkled" in the heading. This
makes that phrase, "*chōji ni kuromu made sosogitaru koto*," very close to the phrase in *SNKS* and *SNKZ*.
NKBT uses the verb *shimikaeritaru* ("dyed deeply") instead.

88. See *SNKS* (1:25) only; *KCS* (434). Jōha now notes Sagoromo's action, humming a snatch of
verse. The gloss admits defeat in identifying the apparent allusions. The series' editors have no more
luck. The teams for *SNKZ* (1:35) and *NKBT* (41) offer lengthy discussions of possible allusions. Their
colleague in *SNKS* suggests an *imayō* (modern song), due to the syllable count.

89. See *SNKS* (1:25), *SNKZ* (1:35), and *NKBT* (41); *KCS* (434). Jōha turns to the Sen'yōden Consort.
He quotes the first line of her reply to the poem noted in gloss 62. Her verse reads: "Sinking into
grief / alone I have become weeds / within the mire. / Today I cannot even / cry out with the iris-
roots" (*uki ni nomi shizumu mikuzu to narihatete kyō wa ayame no ne dani nakarezu*); *SNKZ* and *NKBT*
give the final verb as *nagarezu*, making the last line "float with the iris-roots." This verse foreshadows
one by Sagoromo's lover Asukai; see poem 13 in chapter 2 (*hayaki se no*). Jōha explains several puns

(70) that evening (*sono yūsari* その ゆ ふ さ り):
It says that on the fifth, just as he was preparing to go to the palace, he was summoned there [by the Emperor]. [Sagoromo] was thinking of seeing the Sen'yōden [Consort].[90]

(71) to His Lordship his father (*chichi kō* 父公へ):
It says that he has not yet gone to see him today.[91]

(72) in the rooms of the Empress (*Chūgū no onkata ni wa* 中宮の 御かたには):
This is Sagoromo's younger sister, whose mother is Lady Bōmon, the daughter of the Princely Minister of Ceremonial. It says that she is suffering from some illness, perhaps a cold, and [Lord Horikawa] has yet to visit her. Horikawa, too, is reportedly sick, and he plans to visit her the following morning, once he has recovered. It also says that he thinks she should be able to come home from the palace, given the heat, but it is apparently difficult for her to get leave.[92]

(73) why (*nani shi ni* 何し に):
The two of them grumble that it is miserable to be summoned in this heat. (*An uchiwa is a fan.*)[93]

---

and the general sentiment. *SMKR* conveys the wordplay by using Chinese characters from different levels of meaning: "tears," not "root" (*ne*); but "do not float" rather than "cannot cry" (*nakarenu* and *nagarenu*, respectively). The gloss in *KCS* is simpler and consistent with its practice of writing out Sino-Japanese: "It means that a sinking body cannot readily shed tears. Roots, too, do not float."

90. See *SNKS* (1:25) and, more loosely, *SNKZ* (1:36) and *NKBT* (41); *KCS* (434). I have slightly reformatted the entry, ignoring an awkward space in *SMKR* that creates three sections (the first break comes in the middle of the compound word "palace visit"). Jōha quotes Sagoromo's thoughts as he considers going to the palace. In the series, this skips a line about the Sen'yōden Consort's feelings for Sagoromo, recounted after her verse. Jōha clarifies Sagoromo's intentions, ambiguous in the series. *KCS* contains an interlinear gloss with the Chinese characters for "Sen'yōden."

91. See—approximately—*SNKS* (1:25), *SNKZ* (1:36), and *NKBT* (41); *KCS* (434). The heading, which does not appear in the versions of the tale consulted here, uses an honorific label seen in titles from the second genealogical chart. Jōha presumably quotes from the description of Sagoromo's visit to his father, made before going to court and narrated right after the passage just discussed. The series give *tono no onmae ni* ("before His Lordship"), not specifying the parental relationship. Jōha explains why Sagoromo stops to see his father before going to the palace. *KCS* adds "today, too" (*kyō mo*), implying delinquency on the part of these filial visits.

92. See *SNKS* (1:26) only; *KCS* (434). *SNKZ* (1:36) and *NKBT* (41) have "princess" (*miya*), although the same commoner is meant. Jōha quotes from later in the same passage. Having reported that he is going to the palace, Sagoromo asks if Horikawa has a message for his (the hero's) sister. Jōha identifies her and gives Horikawa's reply. *KCS* has the first phrase of the gloss as its own sentence. The sister's inability to get leave implies the emperor's attachment.

93. See *SNKS* (1:26), *SNKZ* (1:36), and *NKBT* (41); *KCS* (434). Jōha skips ahead slightly, with Sagoromo now alone and muttering about the emperor's frequent summons. Lady Horikawa overhears and suggests that an attendant fan him. Jōha quotes the hero's complaint, then notes that both characters complain. The interlinear note identifies the phonetic transcription for fan and the Chinese character used to write it. *KCS* presents the interlinear note as a separate comment.

(74) *zōgan* (さうがん):
Unknown.[94]

(75) *fusenryo* (ふせんれう):
Raised damask.[95]

(76) at the palace (*uchi ni* 内に):
This must be [due to] loneliness during the rains without the seasonal banquet and so forth.[96]

(77) the Great Minister (*Ōki otodo* 大おとど):
Currently the Provisional Middle Counselor. The person who, as the First Major Counselor in book 4, sets his sights on the Ippon Princess and becomes involved with the attendant Chūnagon, speaking of wet robes. He is the Master of the Crown Prince's Household.[97]

(78) the Left Military Guards (*Sahyōe* 左兵衛):
The Middle Counselor's younger brother. The Consultant Captain, son of the Left Major Captain and the brother of the Sen'yōden [Consort]. They are linked branches.[98]

---

94. See *SNKS* (1:26), *SNKZ* (1:37), and *NKBT* (42); *KCS* (434). Jōha discusses the same passage, with Lady Horikawa admiring her son's clothing—either after seeing him off or before he leaves. The heading flags a confusing term. Jōha admits defeat as to the meaning. The *KCS* editors also seem stumped; they give *sōkan*, while the series' editors add diacritical marks for *zōgan*, literally "elephant eye" patterns worked in gold and silver. These decorate Sagoromo's shift, worn beneath a deeper scarlet robe.

95. See *SNKS* (1:26), *SNKZ* (1:37), and *NKBT* (42); *KCS* (434). Jōha now notes the hero's trousers. The cloth is a kind of purple; as the *NKBT* editors explain, color varied with the wearer's age. Jōha names the weave in phonetic transcription. He also supplies the Chinese characters for it: literally, "floating line damask." This featured raised patterns, here Chinese pinks (*Kara nadeshiko*).

96. See *SNKS* (1:27), *SNKZ* (1:37), and *NKBT* (42); *KCS* (434). The series give "palace" with the compound read *dairi*. Jōha skips ahead to the scene at court, bypassing an interesting and (in the second two series) notably extended discussion of the feelings of Lady Horikawa and her staff. With the usual banquet for the Sweet Flag Festival canceled (no reason appears in my copies), the Crown Prince is visiting the Emperor. The latter has summoned a group of young courtiers to help liven things up. Jōha explains the forced gaiety. The rainy season, mid-June by the modern calendar, was proverbially a time of emotional malaise; the rain made travel unpleasant, and there was a nominal taboo on romance related to the rice-planting season. People were supposed to save their strength for agricultural labor (not done by aristocrats). *KCS* ends the heading with the particle *wa*, also in the series.

97. See *SNKS* (1:27), *SNKZ* (1:37), and *NKBT* (42); *KCS* (434). The series give the Chinese characters for *dajōdaijin* here, read as above. Jōha actually refers to the man's son, one of the young courtiers described in the previous comment. Jōha places him in the larger arc of the tale, as well as within the bureaucracy of the fictional court. The "First Major Counselor" (*Ichi no dainagon*) is presumably the ranking counselor on the Left. *KCS* contains a supplementary note, stating that the final piece of information given in the gloss is mistaken; it is the courtier's younger brother who serves the Crown Prince.

98. See *SNKS* (1:27), *SNKZ* (1:37), and *NKBT* (42); *KCS* (434). Jōha considers the next two courtiers in the group at court. I have reformatted it, following *KCS*; *SMKR* presents the information as a

(79) the Minamoto Middle Captain (*Gen chūjō* 源中将):
This is Sagoromo.[99]

(80) at tonight's banquet (*koyoi no en ni wa* こよひのえんには):
It is the Emperor's command that they play individually, rather than in ensemble.[100]

(81) *This is the person, in the crowd visiting his sister, who drew a picture of Amewakamiko on the night that the Major Captain was eavesdropping at the Kokiden [apartments].*[101]

(82) in particular (*naka ni mo* 中にも):
It says that Sagoromo never even studied the transverse flute casually, so he is startled by the command to play individually.[102]

---

genealogical chart with a short postscript. That combination invites confusion by linking unrelated courtiers and upending the normal visual hierarchy; the chart is drawn as if the Commander (*kami*) of the Left Palace Guards (the series and *KCS* specify this detail) is the father of the Middle Counselor and so on, with the Consultant Captain ultimately placed as the father of both his father and his sister. "Linked branches" (*renshi*) describes noble siblings. *KCS* uses an interlinear note specifying that the Middle Counselor holds a "provisional" (*gon*) post.

99. See *SNKS* (1:27), *SNKZ* (1:37), and *NKBT* (42); *KCS* (434). Jōha quotes the label used for Sagoromo in this passage, then identifies him by his sobriquet. As the *SNKS* editor notes, the label reminds us that Sagoromo's father was born a prince and demoted to commoner status. This further distinguishes the hero from the crowd of elite courtiers just discussed.

100. See *SNKS* (1:27), *SNKZ* (1:38), and *NKBT* (42); *KCS* (434–35). Jōha quotes from the Saga Emperor's initial address to the group under discussion since gloss 76. The content of this speech varies among the series: in *SNKS*, the emperor tells them to demonstrate their full talents on their preferred type of instrument, one song at a time; in *SNKZ*, to play their hearts out, again on their preferred instrument, whether zither or flute; and in *NKBT*, simply to play their hearts out on flutes and zithers. Jōha's digest is closest to the first version. In the series, the Saga Emperor addresses the group again shortly after this; that speech, too, begins with *koyoi* (tonight). Unlike this passage, it concerns his anxiety over Sagoromo's unearthly gifts. However, the related gloss (83) treats something else. Either Jōha's text is different, or he has other priorities.

101. Figure 3 appears at the head of this gloss. See *SNKS* (1:27) and *SNKZ* (1:38) (the latter corrected by the editors); *KCS* (435). In place of the Princely Minister of Central Affairs, *NKBT* (42) gives the Princely Minister of Ceremonial, referenced in glosses 22 and 72. Either way, Jōha quotes from the description of another courtier. Both versions of *Undersash* consulted here present this information as a family tree, including a character who does not enter the tale until much later: the Minor Captain's sister, the doppelganger for the Genji Princess noted in the introduction. The gloss that follows this chart notes another episode referencing Amewakamiko (see gloss 37); it also evokes the Second Princess, via an incidental reference to her Kokiden apartments. See *SNKS* (1:135–36), *SNKZ* (1:170–71), and *NKBT* (125–27) for the initial passage, involving the woman noted above and her painting of Amewakamiko's visit. The Major Captain is Sagoromo, not yet at that rank. Both details look ahead to the consequences of the impending concert. *KCS* includes an immediately relevant detail: the Minor Captain plays the *shō*, a bamboo instrument with vertical pipes.

102. See *SNKS* (1:28) only; *KCS* (435). Jōha seems to skip over the Saga Emperor's second, explicit command that the courtiers perform individually (see gloss 80) as well as the courtiers' own complaints. Instead, he refers to the hero's discomfort at being singled out. The gloss restates Sagoromo's excuse to the emperor but not an important detail present in the series: the emperor has assigned instruments, based on accounts of each courtier's expertise. In *SNKZ* (1:38) and *NKBT* (43), the recalcitrant nobles, led by the provisional counselor, insist that hearing Sagoromo play alone should

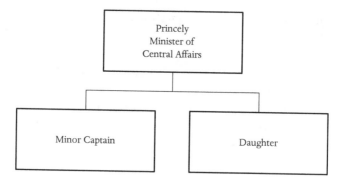

FIGURE 3. A family from the tale.

(83) tonight (*koyoi* こよひ):

The emperor commands him to play it for the first time tonight.[103]

(84) like this (*ito kabakari* no いとかばかりの):

This means that the Emperor does not think that he will ignore a command like this. He says that he has always loved [the hero] just as much as the Minister, and that to oppose his wishes in even something like this is perverse. At this point, [Sagoromo] obeys and picks up the transverse flute.[104]

(85) the others (*koto hitobito mo* こと人々も):

They say that since they cannot match Sagoromo on even his fourth- or fifth-best instruments, the zither and such seem beyond them, no matter what the Emperor says; they ask him to give Sagoromo the zither in their place. The Emperor commands that, since [the hero] is this stubborn about even the transverse flute [they must perform as directed].[105]

---

be good enough. *SNKS* (1:29) gives a similar passage; however, its extended account of the episode stands out. If Jōha is using a similar text, his discussion again seems idiosyncratic.

103. See *SNKS* (1:28), *SNKZ* (1:39), and *NKBT* (43); *KCS* (435). Jōha quotes from the Saga Emperor's curt reply to the hero. The gloss summarizes the rest of it. While the wording varies in the series, the substance of the remark is familiar to any parent of a reluctant performer: "I'm telling you that you must start [playing] tonight" (*koyoi hajimu beki nari,* SNKS); "This time ["tonight, for the first time"] I will make you learn myself" (*koyoi hajimete ware narawasan,* SNKZ and NKBT).

104. See—approximately—*SNKS* (1:28), *SNKZ* (1:40), and *NKBT* (43); *KCS* (435). Jōha quotes from the Saga Emperor's angry rejoinder to Sagoromo's second refusal to perform. The gloss summarizes the reproof and its effect. I correct the unintelligible *omukare* to *somukare* ("ignore"), given in *KCS*. The comment there begins "It says that" (*to nari*) rather than "It means" (*nari*).

105. See—approximately—*SNKS* (1:29), *SNKZ* (1:40), and *NKBT* (44); *KCS* (435). I substitute the repetition-marker used in *KCS* for the vertical version in *SMKR*. This comment is mysterious. While the phrase in the heading appears there, the line discussed in the gloss only appears in *SNKS* and not

(86) had I known it would be like this (*kō to shiramashikaba* かうとしら
ましかば):
In his heart, the Middle Captain thinks that if [he had known that]
the Emperor wants to hear his flute and so on, he should not have
come to the palace, and so he deliberately plays like a novice.[106]

(87) the [Saga] Emperor (*Ue wa* うへは):
He is shocked by the captivating [performance]. The [other]
listeners, too, regret hearing so little, but [Sagoromo] says that His
Lordship only taught him casually and refuses to play more.[107]

(88) how deplorable (*ito utate* いとうたて):
The [Saga] Emperor says that [Sagoromo] must lie easily, and that
although [Sagoromo] plays the flute better than the Minister, if he
finds it so painful to perform, he will not order him to continue.[108]

(89) the Grand [Empress] (*Kōtai* 皇太):
The Grand Empress of the Saga Retired Emperor is the younger
sister of a previous emperor.[109]

---

necessarily in the same context. As a result, I am not entirely sure what is happening in the passage under discussion. Jōha clearly returns to the other courtiers. The series describe them as initially excited by the command to perform individually; as the *SNKZ* editors note, solo performances were rare at the palace. Jōha, however, summarizes their nerve-wracked attempt to avoid playing. *SNKS* credits the idea to the Provisional Counselor, noted earlier. Both versions of *Undersash* consulted here assign the first half of the gloss to the emperor, with the honorific verb *ōsu*. I assume a missing contrasting particle (*mo*) after that verb, shifting the phrase to the courtiers.

106. See *SNKS* (1:29), *SNKZ* (1:41), and *NKBT* (44); *KCS* (435). Jōha now gives the hero's viewpoint. The heading quotes from Sagoromo's thoughts, although their content differs across copies: *SNKS* has Sagoromo feeling *kuyashi*, "regretful" or "annoyed," while the others (almost identical throughout this passage) describe him as *wabishi*, "miserable." Jōha clarifies that these feelings remain unspoken and notes Sagoromo's stratagem. *KCS* further emphasizes the trick with *fukinashitamau*, "plays as if." This verb (not *fukitamau*) adds a third layer of guile to the description.

107. See *SNKS* (1:29) and—approximately—*SNKZ* (1:41) and *NKBT* (44); *KCS* (435). Jōha now discusses Sagoromo's audience. In the latter two series, this includes the rest of the court (*ue o hajimetatematsurite*); *SNKS* describes the response of the others separately. Jōha summarizes the collective response as well as Sagoromo's attempt to stop here.

108. See *SNKS* (1:30), *SNKZ* (1:41), and *NKBT* (44); *KCS* (435). Jōha quotes a line about the Saga Emperor. The deployment of the phrase in the heading differs across the versions of the tale treated here: in *SNKS*, it prefaces the remark discussed in the gloss (*SNKS*: "How deplorable! You are even good at lying"); in the others, it expresses a more general sentiment ("Lies are deplorable"). Jōha summarizes this latest reproof—as usual in *Undersash*, with a specific reference to imperial speech (*chokugen*). The special status of the emperor also shows in the previous entry, which distinguishes him from Sagoromo's "listeners" (*kiku hitobito*).

109. See *SNKS* (1:30), *SNKZ* (1:42), and *NKBT* (45); *KCS* (435). Jōha identifies another member of the audience, the Saga Empress. In the series, the passage actually concerns her daughters, including the Second Princess. Their presence makes the hero more nervous. (In *SNKZ* and *NKBT*, tension is already high after an additional complaint by the emperor, who insists that tonight he will finally purge his resentment by hearing all he likes of the hero's music; see p. 41 and p. 44, respectively.) Jōha only discusses the empress, perhaps due to her unusual title. It was originally used for the dowager empress—that is, the mother of the current emperor. However, it came to signify the senior empress

(90) His Lordship (*Otodo no* おとどの):

The Middle Captain must think that [Lord Horikawa] would find this inauspicious. The "sleeves" must be those of the Son of Heaven.[110]

(91) the *hatate* of the clouds (*kumo no hatate* 雲のはたて):

These are clouds trailing like banners.[111]

(92) lightning (*inazuma no* いなづまの):

Just when they think it will thunder, music sounds throughout the sky.[112]

(93) *asami* (*asami* あさみ):

Commonly, this was called *asamu* [to marvel]. This word also appears in *Genji*.[113]

(94) "lightning" poem (*inazuma no uta* いなづまの哥):

It must mean that he wants to cross a bridge of clouds in order to perform with [the heavenly musicians].[114]

---

in the reign of Go-Reizei (see Jōha's first chart), who gave multiple consorts the title of empress, *chūgū*. *KCS* uses the full title, *kōtaigōgū*, as the heading.

110. See *SNKS* (1:31), *SNKZ* (1:42), and *NKBT* (45); *KCS* (435). None of the series includes the particle *no*, presumably used here as a subject marker. Jōha seems to skip an intriguing initial description of Sagoromo's performance; given the strange resonance of his flute and the hero's special radiance amid even bright torches and moonlight, his audience wonders uneasily if anything else might be watching him. Instead, Jōha quotes from the beginning of Sagoromo's own surmise about what his father would think if he were present. (As noted in gloss 72, Lord Horikawa is nursing a cold at home.) Jōha then summarizes the hero's conclusion and clarifies the subjects of each part of the sentence, narrated slightly differently in each of the texts considered here. (*NKBT* assigns the tear-soaked sleeves to Sagoromo.) *KCS* has the particle *wa* after the first phrase of the gloss.

111. See *SNKS* (1:31) and *SNKZ* (1:43); *KCS* (435). *NKBT* (45) has *sora no hate*. Jōha quotes from what is in the series the second description of Sagoromo's performance. It begins with the strains of his flute echoing throughout the sky; from here through gloss 98, see chapter 4. As Laurel Rodd notes in her translation of a poem that the *SNKS* and *SNKZ* editors cite in their own gloss, *kumo no hatate* may mean either "end of the clouds" or "banners of cloud" (*Kokinshū*, 188). Jōha indicates the second option using Chinese characters.

112. See *SNKS* (1:31), *SNKZ* (1:43), and *NKBT* (45); *KCS* (435–36). Jōha again quotes from the description of Sagoromo's performance, which now provokes flashes of lightning and increasing misgivings in his audience; again, see chapter 4. The gloss notes the general confusion and the amazing truth. *KCS* does not include the particle at the end of the heading.

113. See *SNKS* (1:31) and—approximately—*SNKZ* (1:43) and *NKBT* (45); *KCS* (436). In the first text, the word in the heading appears in the phrase *asamisawagasetamō*; the other series use a related adjective, *asamashi*, but in different phrases (*asamashū oboshimeshi sawagasetamau* and *asamashiku oboshisawagasetamau*, respectively). All of these describe the uproar at court. Jōha gives a vernacular equivalent for the verb and ties it broadly to *Genji*.

114. See *SNKS* (1:32), *SNKZ* (1:43), and *NKBT* (46); *KCS* (436). Jōha quotes the first line of Sagoromo's poem, presumably recited in his head as he redoubles his efforts on his flute. For the text and translation, see the notes to "Sagoromo's Sleeves" in chapter 3 (*inazuma no*). Jōha explains that the poem expresses Sagoromo's wish to participate in the celestial performance. The series' editors, by contrast, take the hero at his word; they read the verse as his bid to quit the court. The *SNKS* editor has him addressing the clouds, while the others see the verse as meant for the heavens at large. *KCS* gives the character for "poem" at the start of the gloss rather than in the heading, and follows it with a second statement that this is the hero's verse (*Sagoromo no uta nari*) before offering the interpretation seen above.

(95) thread-play (*itoyū* いとゆふ):
[Amewakamiko's robe] looks something like threads scattered in sunlight.[115]

(96) he, too (*ware mo* 我も):
It says that even Sagoromo feels lonely at the thought of being taken away.[116]

(97) sadly (*kanashiku* かなしく):
Here Sagoromo says words to the effect that while he thinks of this world with distaste, when he considers the feelings of the [Saga] Emperor and his parents, he cannot go [with Amewakamiko].[117]

(98) cloud *koshi* (*kumo no koshi* 雲のこし):
Cloud carriage. *This should be looked into.*[118]

(99) with concern (*ayauku* あやうく):
This is the [Saga] Emperor's thought. He is considering how to keep Sagoromo's mind fixed on earth.[119]

---

115. See *SNKS* (1:32), *SNKZ* (1:44), and *NKBT* (46); *KCS* (436). In the series, Jōha skips past the actual descent and description of the deity (immediately identified in *SNKZ* and *NKBT* as Amewakamiko) to quote the description of his robe: in *SNKS*, "a light robe that looked like the shimmering of hot air [i.e., a heat mirage] or some such thing" (*itoyū ka nanzo to miyuru usuki koromo*; *NKBT* has *itoyū no yō naru mono*, "something like a shimmering of hot air"; *SNKZ* splits the difference with *itoyū no yō naru usuki koromo*, "a light robe like the shimmering of hot air"). I borrow this beautiful translation of *itoyū* from jisho.org. The term is written with the Chinese characters for "thread" and "play." Jōha explains the word in these terms, while gesturing toward the heat.

116. See *SNKS* (1:32) and—approximately—*SNKZ* (1:44) and *NKBT* (46); *KCS* (436). The latter two series give *ware wa*. This is another striking gloss. Instead of noting Amewakamiko's attempt to put his robe on the hero—which would give Sagoromo the power to ascend to the heavens, fulfilling the wish expressed in his earlier poem— Jōha quotes Sagoromo's reaction. The series describe this variously; *SNKZ* and *NKBT* are as usual much closer to each other than to *SNKS*, apparently closest to Jōha's text. Jōha attributes Sagoromo's feelings—in *SNKS*, "extreme loneliness" (*imijiku monogokoroboshi*)—to his realization that the god might take him away forever. The *SNKS* editor paraphrases differently, saying that Sagoromo is beside himself with shock.

117. See *SNKS* (1:33) only; *KCS* (456). This part of the episode varies significantly in *SNKS* and the version presented in *SNKZ* (1:44–45) and *NKBT* (46–47). Among other things, the latter two series paraphrase an exchange of Chinese poems in which Amewakamiko, noting the Saga Emperor's distress, announces that he cannot take Sagoromo home with him; Sagoromo, referring to the ties that bind him to the world (*hodashi*), states that he cannot go. In *SNKS*, which does not mention any words from the deity, the heading corresponds to a much lengthier paraphrase of Sagoromo's refusal to ascend to the heavens, again reportedly expressed in Chinese verse. Jōha seems to summarize a similar passage. Assuming that his text remains close to *SNKS*, he skips another description of the emperor's response to these events, which speculates about the hero.

118. See *SNKS* (1:33), *SNKZ* (1:45), and *NKBT* 47; *KCS* (436). Jōha quotes from the description of Amewakamiko's vehicle, not mentioned earlier in the episode. The gloss clarifies the meaning of the second word (first presented in *hiragana*). While the supplementary comment suggests uncertainty, the *SNKZ* and *NKBT* editors note several earlier examples of the phrase in other court tales; there it indicates the conveyance of gods and buddhas, with the *NKBT* team specifying that the phrase serves as a metaphor for the clouds on which celestial beings descend to earth. *KCS* gives the gloss in one piece: *unkyō tazunubeshi*.

119. See *SNKS* (1:34), *SNKZ* (1:46), and *NKBT* (47); *KCS* (456). The first two series give *ayafuku*, the standard spelling, which the *NKBT* editors provide as a gloss. Only *SNKS* contains a line similar to that discussed in the second half of Jōha's comment. Jōha seems to skip Sagoromo's grief at

(100) the First Princess (*Ichi no miya wa* 一宮は):

> The Kamo Priestess; both the [Saga] Emperor and her mother, the [Saga] Empress, love the Second Princess best. The Son of Heaven thinks of offering her to Sagoromo as a personal substitute for the night that Amewakamiko descended, but because [Sagoromo] is in love with the Genji Princess, he does not accept. On the night that he peeks in at the Kokiden [apartments], he sees [the Second Princess], and after Sagoromo's secret visit she gives birth to the young prince. Her mother announces that the child is her own. When [the Empress] dies from grief seven days later, the [Second Princess] is horrified and pleads illness to take the tonsure.[120]

Amewakamiko's departure, to quote from a description of the Saga Emperor's fear that the hero will regret staying at court. The passage in the modern series is unclear; it alternates between the emperor's reflections and his surmise of Sagoromo's own feelings. Jōha notes the emperor's resolve to redirect Sagoromo's attention "to this world" (*kono yo ni* [*Sagoromo no kokoro todomen*]). In *SNKS*, the related line has the emperor worrying that at this point the hero may no longer be interested in this world (*itodo kono yo ni kokoro todomezu ya narinamu*); this negative phrasing resembles *KCS*.

120. *SNKS* (1:34); *SNKZ* (1:46) has the abbreviated *ichi wa*, while *NKBT* (47) gives *hitori wa* "one of them." Jōha quotes from the Saga Emperor's meditation on how to keep Sagoromo on earth. Jōha skips over the initial thought of promoting the hero, quickly discarded, to highlight the emperor's decision to give Sagoromo one of his daughters. Jōha's heading reminds us of the gap between *SNKS* and his text. In *SNKZ* and *NKBT*, the emperor first thinks of his oldest daughter, the First Princess, and it is this character that Jōha names in the heading; he presumably marks the start of this important passage in his own copy of the tale. *SNKS* begins with the emperor's thoughts of the Second Princess (specifically, of her beauty), and only then turns to the formal consideration of the two sisters by birth order. In the gloss, Jōha quickly identifies the First Princess by her current office and then offers a lengthy introduction to the Second Princess. As those comments make clear, he treats her very differently than her sister, summarizing her life. There is an interlinear note next to "mother" highlighting the latter's rank. *KCS* (436) splits the information found above into two glosses. The first entry, given under the heading listed above, says "Kamo Priestess" (perhaps meaning the Ippon Princess; see the introduction). The second entry, headed "this princess" (*kono miya o ba*) begins with the phrase "this the First Princess" (presumably a mistake for "Second Princess"). It then lists everything else, with the honorific glyph preceding "mother" embedded in the gloss.

Appendix A

List of *Sagoromo*-Themed Poems

All of the poems listed below appear in full or partial quotation in at least one of the medieval tributes translated here. Those quoted in part are given in full in the notes. Where there are variants, I use the text cited in my translation. When I do not cite the full poem in translation, I quote the Japanese version found in *SNKS*.

Aimite wa sode nuremasaru sayogoromo hitoyo bakari mo hedatezu mogana

Aki no iro wa sa mo koso mieme tanomeshi o matanu inochi no tsuraku mo
   aru kana

Ama no to o yasurai ni koso ideshika to yūtsukedori yo towaba kotaeyo

Asukagawa asu wataran to omou ni mo kyō no hiruma wa nao zo koishiki

Asukai ni kage mimahoshiki yadori shite mimagusa gakure hito ya togamen

Asukai no mizu ni yadoreru tsuki nareba kumori ari to wa tare ka mirubeki

Aware sou aki no tsukikage sode narade ōkata ni nomi nagame ya wa suru

Chigiri araba mata mo kon'yo ni meguriawan kyō wa fuchise ni mi o ba iru to mo

Fujigoromo kitaru mi nareba kakure nashi orikemu hito o tare to toekashi

Fukiharau yomo no kogarashi kokoro araba ukimi o kakusu kuma mo araseyo

Furusato wa asajigahara ni narihatete mushi no ne shigeki aki ni zo aramashi

Hakanaku mo kyō wa fuchise ni irinu to mo nakaran ato o tare ka towamashi

Hayaki se no soko no mikuzu to nariniki to ōgi no kaze ni fuki mo tsutaeyo

Hikitsurete kyō wa kazashishi aoigusa omoi mo kakenu shime no hoka kana

Hito shirenu irie no sawa ni shiru hito mo naku naku kisuru tsuru no kegoromo

Hito shirezu osauru sode mo shiboru made shigure to tomo ni furu namida kana

Ika ni semu iwanu iro naru hana nareba kokoro no uchi o shiru hito mo nashi

Inazuma no hikari ni yukamu ama no hara haruka ni watase kumo no kakehashi

Inochi sae tsuki sezu mono o omou kana wakareshi hodo ni tae mo hatenade

Iro iro ni kasanete wa kiji hito shirezu omoisometeshi yowa no sagoromo

Iwabashi o yoru yoru dani mo watarabaya taema ya okan Kazuragi no kami

Kajio tae inochi mo tayu to shirasebaya namida no umi ni shizumu funabito

Kamiyo yori shimehiki yuishi sakakiba o ware yori hoka ni tare ka orubeki

Katashiki ni kasaneshi koromo uchikaeshi omoeba nani o kouru kokoro zo

Kawaraji to iishi shiishiba machimibaya Tokiwa no mori ni aki ya miyuru to

Koe tatete nakanu bakari zo mono omou mi wa utsusemi ni otori ya wa suru

Koite naku namida ni kumoru tsukikage wa yadoru sode mo ya nururu kao naru
Koiwataru tamoto wa itsumo kawakanu ni kyō wa ayame no ne sae nakarete
Koto no ha o nao ya tanomamu hashitaka no Tokaeru yama wa momiji
    shinu to mo
Kumoi made oinoboranamu tane makishi hito mo tazunenu mine no wakamatsu
Kuyashiku mo aketekeru kana maki no to o yasurai ni koso arubekarikere
Mate shibashi yama no ha meguru tsuki dani mo ukiyo ni ware o todomezaranamu
Mi mo wakade suginikeru ka na oshinabete noki no ayame no hima shi nakereba
Minashigo to hane naki tori to kurabureba nao minashigo zo kanashikarikeru
Mi no shiro mo ware nugikisen kaeshitsu to omoi na wabi so ama no hagoromo
Misogi suru yao yorozu yo no kami mo kike moto yori tare ka omoisometeshi
Moewataru wagami zo Fuji no yama yo tada yuki ni mo kiezu keburi tachitsutsu
Murasaki no mi no shiro goromo sore naraba otome no sode ni masari koso seme
Nagaraete araba au yo o matsubeki ni inochi wa tsukinu hito wa toikozu
Nagarete mo ause ari ya to mi o nagete Mushiake no seto ni machi kokoro mimu
Namidagawa nagaruru ato wa sore nagara shigarami tomuru omokage zo naki
Nao tanomu Tokiwa no mori no makibashira wasure na hate so kuchi wa
    shinu to mo
Omoiki ya mugura no kado o yukisugite kusa no makura ni tabine semu to wa
Omoitsutsu Iwagakinuma no ayamegusa migomorinagara kuchi ya hatenamu
Omoiyaru kokoro izuku ni ainuramu umiyama to dani shiranu wakare ni
Omokage wa mi o zo hanarenu uchitokete nenu yo no yume wa miru to nakeredo
Orekaeri okifushi waburu shitaogi no sue kosu kaze o hito no toekashi
Sakakiba ni kakaru kokoro o ika ni sen oyobanu eda to omoitayuredo
Seku sode ni morite namida ya sometsuramu kozue iro masu aki no yūgure
Shikitae no makura zo ukite nagarekeru imo naki toko no aki no nezame ni
Shinikaeri matsu ni inochi zo taenubeki naka naka nani ni tanomisomekemu
Shiranuma no ayame wa sore to miezu to mo yomogi ga kado wa sugizu mo
    aranamu
Shirazarishi ashi no mayoi no tazu no ne o kumo no ue ni ya kikiwatarubeki
Shitaogi ni tsuyu kiewabishi yona yona mo toubeki mono to matare ya wa seshi
Sue no yo mo chigiri ya wa suru kuretake no uwaba no yuki o nani tanomuramu
Sue no yo mo nani tanomuramu take no ha ni kakareru yuki no kie mo hatenade
Tachikaeri orade sugi uki ominaeshi nao yasurawan kiri no magaki ni
Tani fukami tatsu odamaki wa ware nare ya omou kokoro no kuchite yaminuru
Tanomekoshi izura Tokiwa no mori ya kore hito tanome naru na ni koso arikere
Tanometsutsu iku yo henuramu take no ha ni furu shirayuki no kiekaeritsutsu
Tazunubeki kusa no hara sae shimogarete tare ni towamashi michishiba no tsuyu
Tomare to mo e koso iwarene Asukai ni yadorihatsubeki kage shi nakereba
Ukifune no tayori ni yukamu watatsuumi no soko to oshieyo ato no shiranami

Ukimi ni wa aki zo shirareshi ogihara ya sue kosu kaze no oto naranedomo

Uki ni nomi shizumu mikuzu to narihatete kyō wa ayame no ne dani nakarezu

Ukishizumi ne nomi nagaruru ayamegusa kakaru koiji to hito mo shiranu ni

Utatane o naka naka yume to omowabaya samete awasuru hito mo ari ya to

Waga kokoro kanete sora ni ya michinuramu yuku kata shiranu yado no kayaribi

Wakikaeri kōri no shita wa musebitsutsu sa mo wabisasuru Yoshinogawa kana

Ware bakari omoikogarete toshi fu ya to Muro no yashima no keburi ni mo toe

Ware bakari omoi shi mo seji fuyu no yo ni tsugawanu oshi no ukine nari to mo

Yomosugara mono ya omoeru hototogisu ama no iwato o akegata ni naku

Yomosugara nageki akashite hototogisu naku ne o dani mo kiku hito mogana

Yoshi saraba mukashi no ato o tazune miyo ware nomi mayou koi no michi ka wa

Yukusue mo tanomi ya wa suru take no ha ni kakareru yuki no ikuyo to mo nashi

Yuku sue o tanomu to mo naki inochi ni te mada iwane naru matsu ni wakaruru

Yume ka to yo mishi ni mo nitaru tsurasa kana uki wa tameshi mo araji to
omou ni

Appendix B

Resources for Further Study

Locations and Descriptions of Additional Tributes

Kawasaki Sachiko. *Sagoromo monogatari kyōju shironkyū*. Kyoto: Shibunkaku Shuppan, 2010.

In addition to my default version of *Sagoromo no shitahimo*, contains transcriptions of four other texts: a copy of *Shitahimo* in the hand of famed calligrapher Konoe Nobutada (1565–1614); a copy of *Sagoromo keizu* in the hand of Konoe Hisatsugu (identified in chapter 5); another copy held by Tokyo University Library's Nanki Bunko; and a copy of *Sagoromo monogatarishō* held by Miyagi Prefecture's Date Bunko.

Komatsu Shigemi. *Ise monogatari emaki. Sagoromo monogatari emaki. Komakurabe gyōkō emaki. Genji monogatari emaki*. Vol. 18 of *Nihon no emaki*. Tokyo: Chūō Kōronsha, 1993.

Contains photographic reproductions of the extant portions of the fourteenth-century picture scroll devoted to the tale.

Nakajō Satoko. *Rufu-bon Sagoromo monogatari to Shitahimo no kenkyū*. Tokyo: Shintensha, 2003.

Contains a photographic reproduction of the *Sagoromo keizu* in the hand of Konoe Hisatsugu (introduced in chapter 5), held by Yōmei Bunko, and transcriptions of the following four texts: the copy of *Shitahimo*, in the hand of Mouri Motoyasu (1560–1601), held by the Imperial Household Agency's Shoryōbu archive; the copy of *Shitahimo* held by Kyoto University's Kikutei Bunko; the copy of *Sagoromo kikigaki* held by Hōsa Bunko; and the copy of *Sagoromo kikigaki* held by Yōmei Bunko.

Nakano Kōichi, ed. *Nara ehon emakishū*. Vol. 12. Tokyo: Waseda Daigaku Shuppanbu, 1988.

Contains photographic reproductions of the texts and some illustrations from two *Sagoromo*-themed tales: a two-volume *Sagoromo no chūjō* and a one-volume *Sagoromo*, both "horizontal books" (*yoko hon*). The former, very close to the text used as my default, contains fifteen illustrations reproduced in black and white. One color reproduction at the front.

Orikuchi Shinobu, ed. *Kokubungaku chūshaku sōsho*. Vol. 15. Tokyo: Meicho Kankōkai, 1930.

In addition to the alternate version of *Sagoromo shitahimo* noted earlier, contains transcriptions of the following three texts: *Sagoromo monogatari mokuroku narabi ni nenjo* by Shaka (Ikkadō) Setsurin (1591–1662); a copy of *Sagoromo monogatari* with interlinear notes by Ishikawa Masamochi (1754–1830) and

Shimizu Hamaomi (1776–1824); and a copy of *Sagoromo keizu* identified as the version by Sanjōnishi Sanetaka.

Sudō Kei. *Sagoromo monogatari juyō no kenkyū*. Tokyo: Shintensha, 2013. Contains transcriptions of the following four texts: *Sagoromo no uta*, included in Shiguretei Bunko's copy of *Kuden waka shakushō*; poems included in Sonkeikaku Bunko's copy of *Ruiku waka shiku*; poems included in the 1666 (Kanbun 6) printing of *Kokon ruiku*; and *Sagoromo waka nukigaki*, included in the 1692 (Genroku 5) copy of *Genji Sagoromo uta*, in the hand of Higashizono Motomasa (1675–1728).

Yokoyama Shigeru, ed. *Muromachi jidai monogatari*. Vol. 7. Tokyo: Koten Bunko, 1966. In addition to the version of *Sagoromo no chūjō* noted earlier, contains transcriptions of three originally illustrated texts: an unpublished, partially colored printed story (*tanrokubon*); a large-size (*ōgata*) illustrated manuscript (*Nara ehon*); and a half-size (*hanshibon*) illustrated manuscript. They are all titled *Sagoromo*.

Yokoyama Shigeru and Matsumoto Ryūshin, eds. *Muromachi jidai monogatari taisei*. Vol. 6. Tokyo: Kadokawa Shoten, 1978. In addition to the same version of *Sagoromo no chūjō* noted earlier, this volume also contains transcriptions of two additional texts: *Sagoromo no taishō* and *Sagoromo*.

Related Research

Egusa Miyuki. "Meisho 'Mushiake' o meguru *Sagoromo monogatari* juyōka." In *Heian bungaku no kochūshaku to juyō*, edited by Jinno Hidenori, Niimi Akihiko, and Yokomizo Hiroshi, 2:215–23. Musashino Shoin, 2009.

——. "Waka ni okeru *Sagoromo monogatari* sesshu no kenkyū: Fujiwara Teika o jiku ni." PhD dissertation, Waseda University, 2014.

Higashino Yasuko. "*Genji Sagoromo utaawase* no ban to sono keisei." *Mozu kokubun* 9 (1989): 20–43.

Hirabayashi Kazunari. *Nō gikyoku kaishaku no kanōsei: Ashikari no nō kara Sagoromo made*. Waseda Daigaku Shuppanbu, 2009.

Ichimonji Akiko. "*Sagoromo monogatari* ni okeru kanbun juyō no hōhō: Den Tameaki hitsu bon to *Shinsen Manyōshū*." *Kokubun mejiro* 53 (2014): 75–86.

Iwagi Kentarō. "Yōkyoku *Sagoromo* no kōsei: Muromachi bungei ni okeru *Sagoromo monogatari* Amewakamiko kōka bamen no juyō no yōsō." In Ningen bunka kenkyūkikō Kokubungaku Kenkyū Shiryōkan bungaku keisei kenkyūkei Heian bungaku ni okeru bamen seisei kenkyū purojekuto, *Monogatari no seisei to juyō*, 2:78–113. Kokubungaku Kenkyū Shiryōkan, 2007.

Katagiri Noboru. "Haikyoku *Sagoromo* memo." *Nō: kenkyū to hyōron* 6 (1976): 27–30.

Kawasaki Sachiko. "Satomura Jōha to Nara renga: *Sagoromo monogatari* juyōshi kenkyū no ichijo to shite." *Machikaneyama ronsō, bungaku hen* 34 (2000): 1–14.

Komeda Akemi. *Fūyō wakashū no kōzō ni kansuru kenkyū*. Kasama Shoin, 2015.

Mashimo Miyako. "*Sagoromo no sōshi* shohon to tenkai to sono bungeisei." *Ritsumeikan bungaku* 505 (1988): 137–59.

Miyazaki Yūko. "*Fūyō wakashū* ni okeru jinbutsu kishō." *Gobun kenkyū* (Kyūshū Daigaku Kokugo Kokubun Gakkai) 113 (2012): 27–39.

Nagaike Kenji. "*Geniyasaba*: Sōka senyō ittai sanmei no hiju to Zenkōji no hijiri." *Kokubungaku kaishaku to kyōzai no kenkyū* 48, no. 6 (2003): 108–17.

Naganuma Tomona. "*Genji Sagoromo hyakuban utaawase* no kenkyū: Kantō kanjiku ni mirareru senshū ishiki." *Nihon bungaku* 111 (2015): 57–71.

Sudō Kei. "*Sagoromo monogatari* kohitsu-gire no hitoyōsō: Den Abutsu-ni hitsu gire, den Reizei Tamesuke hitsu gire, den Kazan'in Morokata hitsu gire kara." *Ronkyū Nihon bungaku* 97 (2012): 21–40.

Tachibana Ritsu. "'*Sagoromo no sōshi*' no ihon to shurui to sono denpon." *Bungaku ronsō* 21 (1961): 32–46.

———. "Zai Pari *Sagoromo no sōshi* ni tsuite: Shodenpon no shurui to kanren shite." *Bungaku ronsō* 59 (1985): 105–19.

Tashiro Keiichi. "Shoryōbu shozō *Sagoromo monogatari* ni tsuite: Nara ehon sakusei jijō no ittan." *Shoryōbu kiyō* 63 (2011): 97–109.

Toyoshima Hidenori. "Monogatari to kayō: *Sagoromo monogatari* ni sokushite." *Kokugakuin zasshi* 110, no. 11 (2009): 107–16.

Yamamoto Miki. "*Genji Sagoromo hyakuban utaawase* no kenkyū: Hairetsu o chūshin ni." *Sōka Daigaku Daigakuin kiyō* 31 (2009): 287–307.

———. "*Genji Sagoromo utaawase* no kōsatsu: Asukai to Yūgao, Ukifune no ban kara." *Sōka Daigaku Daigakuin kiyō* 33 (2011): 197–210.

———. "*Monogatari nihyakuban utaawase* no shiron: Honkadori no shuhō ni miru kyōjisei o tansho to shite." *Nihongo Nihon bungaku* (Sōka Daigaku Nihongo Nihon Bungaku Kai) 23 (2013): 13–27.

———. "*Monogatari nihyakuban utaawase* ron: *Hyakuban utaawase* ni okeru sōi to yūgō." *Nihongo Nihon bungaku* (Sōka Daigaku Nihongo Nihon Bungaku Kai) 24 (2014): 45–59.

BIBLIOGRAPHY

All works in Japanese published in Tokyo unless otherwise noted.

Primary Texts

Haga Yaichi and Sasaki Nobutsuna, eds. *Kōchū yōkyoku sōsho*. Vol. 2. Kyoto: Rinsen Shoten, 1987.

Higuchi Yoshimaro, ed. *Ōchō monogatari shūkasen*. 2 vols. Iwanami Shoten, 1987–89.

Kawasaki Sachiko, ed. "Shiryō hen." In *Sagoromo monogatari kyōjushi ronkyū*, 213–400. Kyoto: Shibunkaku Shuppan, 2010.

Kokumin tosho kabushiki kaisha, ed. *Kōchū kokka taikei*. Vol. 23. Kokumin Tosho, 1930.

Komachiya Teruhiko and Gotō Shōko, eds. *Sagoromo monogatari*. Vols. 29–30 of *SNKZ*. Shōgakkan, 1999.

Kuwabara Hiroshi, ed. *Mumyōzōshi*. Vol. 7 of *SNKS*. Shinchōsha, 1976.

Mitani Ei'ichi and Sekine Yoshiko, eds. *Sagoromo monogatari*. Vol. 79 of *NKBT*. Iwanami Shoten, 1965.

Nakano Kōichi, ed. *Nara ehon emakishū*. Vol. 12. Waseda Daigaku Shuppanbu, 1988.

Nihon meicho zenshū kankōkai, ed. *Yōkyoku sanbyaku-gojūbanshū*. Vol. 29 of *Nihon meicho zenshū* (Edo bungei no bu). Nihon Meicho Zenshū Kankō, 1928.

Orikuchi Shinobu, ed. *Kokubungaku chūshaku sōsho*. Vol. 15. Meicho Kankōkai, 1930.

Suzuki Kazuo, ed. *Sagoromo monogatari*. Vols. 68 and 74 of *SNKS*. Shinchōsha, 1985–86.

Tōgo Yoshida. *Chūko kayō enkyoku zenshū*. Kokusho Kankōkai, 1918.

——, ed. *Enkyoku jūshichi chō Yōkyoku sue hyakuban*. Kokusho Kankōkai, 1912.

Tonomura Hisae and Tonomura Natsuko, eds. *Sōka zenshishū*. Yayoi Shoten, 1993.

Yashima Gakutei. "Deity Listening to a Courtier Playing Flute: The Sagoromo Captain (*Sagoromo no taishō*), from the series *Three Gentlemen of Japanese Literature (Washo sankōshi)*." Circa 1819–20. Woodblock print (*surimono* in *shikishiban* format). Harvard Art Museums. https://www.harvardartmuseums.org/art/207855.

——. "*The Tale of Sagoromo (Sagoromo)*, from the series *Ten Courtly Tales for the Honcho Circle (Honchōren monogatari jūban)*." Circa 1820. Woodblock print (*surimono* in *shikishiban* format). Art Institute of Chicago. https://www.artic.edu/artworks/80931/the-tale-of-sagoromo-from-the-series-ten-courtly-tales-for-the-honcho-circle-honchoren-monogatari-juban.

Yokoyama Shigeru, ed. *Muromachi jidai monogatari*. Vol. 7. Koten Bunko, 1966.

Yokoyama Shigeru and Matsumoto Ryūshin, eds. *Muromachi jidai monogatari taisei*. Vol. 6. Kadokawa Shoten, 1978.

Secondary Sources in Japanese

Fujioka Sakutarō. *Kokubungaku zenshi: Heianchō hen.* Tokyo Kaiseikan, 1905.

Gakushūin Daigaku Heian Bungaku Kenkyūkai, ed. *Sanjōnishi kebon Sagoromo monogatari chūshaku.* Bensei Shuppan, 2019.

Gotō Yasufumi. "*Sagoromo monogatari* sakuchūka no haikei (3)." *Bunken kenkyū* 24 (1989): 48–56.

Kawasaki Sachiko. *Sagoromo monogatari kyōjushi ronkyū.* Kyoto: Shibunkaku Shuppan, 2010.

Mashimo Miyako. "Kinsei-ki no *Sagoromo no sōshi*: Ihon sakusei no hōhō to kyōju." *Ritsumeikan bungaku* 512 (1989): 1–34.

Matsumura Hiroshi and Ishikawa Tōru. "Kaisetsu." In *Sagoromo monogatari,* edited by Matsumura and Ishikawa, Vol. 1, 3–179. Asahi Shimbunsha, 1965.

Oguri Nobuko. "*Monogatari hyakuban utaawase* no kotobagaki to *Fūyō wakashū* no kotobagaki ni tsuite: *Sagoromo monogatari* o chūshin ni." *Aichi Shukutoku Daigaku kokugo kokubun* 15 (1992): 71–81.

Okuda Isao. *Rengashi: Sono kōdō to bungaku.* Hyōronsha, 1976.

Sudō Kei. *Sagoromo monogatari juyō no kenkyū.* Shintensha, 2013.

Sugiura Noriko. "*Sagoromo monogatari* ni okeru waka no igi: Sanbun to no sōgō kankei." *Sugiyama kokubungaku* 1 (1977): 21–34.

Takahashi Tōru. "*Sagoromo monogatari* genzon ega shiryō bamen ichiran." In *Sagoromo monogatari zenchūshaku,* edited by Sagoromo Monogatari Kenkyūkai, 5:431–43. Ōfū, 2010.

Tanaka Takeshi. *Kiku to aoi: Go-Mizunoo tennō to Tokagawa sandai no sōkoku.* Yumani Shobō, 2012.

Toki Takeji. "*Sagoromo monogatari* bōtō no issetsu ni tsuite." *Ronkyū Nihon bungaku* 12 (1960): 10–17.

Tonomura Natsuko. "Sōka ni okeru monogatari-kayōka no hōhō: *Sagoromo no sode, Sagoromo no tsuma* wo chūshin ni." *Kokugo to kokubungaku* 47, no. 5 (1970): 14–26.

Toyoshima Hidenori. "Koromo no keifu: Sagoromo, sayogoromo, koke no koromo." *Hirosaki Gakuin Daigaku kiyō* 18 (1982): 11–21.

——. "Monogatari to kayō: *Sagoromo monogatari* ni sokushite." *Kokugakuin zasshi* 110, no. 11 (2009): 107–16.

Ueno Eiko. "Jōha no baai: *Sagoromo no shō* kara *Sagoromo no shitahimo* e no tenkai." In *Genji monogatari e Genji monogatari kara,* edited by Nagai Kazuko, 474–501. Kasama Shoin, 2007.

Secondary Sources in English

Atkins, Paul S. *Teika: The Life and Works of a Medieval Japanese Poet.* Honolulu: University of Hawai'i Press, 2017.

Boot, W. J. "The Death of a Shogun: Deification in Early Modern Japan." In *Shinto in History: Ways of the Kami,* edited by John Breen and Mark Teeuwen, 144–66. Honolulu: University of Hawai'i Press, 2000.

Brazell, Karen, trans. *The Confessions of Lady Nijō.* Stanford: Stanford University Press, 1973.

Brooks, Douglas. "Japanese Wooden Boatbuilding: History and Traditions." *Education about Asia* 19.2 (2014): 85–87.

Brown, Delmer M., and Ichirō Ishida. *The Future and the Past: A Translation and Study of the Gukanshō, an Interpretative History of Japan Written in 1219.* Berkeley: University of California Press, 1979.

Butler, Lee. "The Riches of Medieval Japanese Society." Review of *The World Turned Upside Down: Medieval Japanese Society*, by Pierre Souyri (trans. Käthe Roth). H-Japan, H-Net: Humanities & Social Sciences Online, June 1, 2002. https://networks.h-net.org/node/20904/reviews/21131/butler-souyri-world-turned-upside-down-medieval-japanese-society.

Bynner, Witter. *The Jade Mountain: A Chinese Anthology, Being Three Hundred Poems of the T'ang Dynasty, 618–906.* New York: Alfred A. Knopf, 1920.

Carter, Steven D. *Haiku before Haiku: From the Renga Masters to Bashō.* New York: Columbia University Press, 2011.

———. *How to Read a Japanese Poem.* New York: Columbia University Press, 2019.

Chan, Timothy Wai Keung. "Dedication and Identification in Wang Bo's Compositions on the Gallery of Prince Teng." *Monumenta Serica* 50 (2002): 215–55.

Childs, Margaret H. *Rethinking Sorrow: Revelatory Tales of Late Medieval Japan.* Ann Arbor: Center for Japanese Studies, The University of Michigan, 1991.

Cranston, Edwin A. *A Waka Anthology.* Vol. 2, *Grasses of Remembrance.* Stanford: Stanford University Press, 2006.

D'Etcheverry, Charo. *Love after "The Tale of Genji": Rewriting the World of the Shining Prince.* Cambridge, MA: Harvard University Asia Center, 2007.

———. "Out of the Mouths of Nurses." *Monumenta Nipponica* 59, no. 2 (2004): 153–77.

———. "Performing Emotion: Miracles, Postscripts, and *Waka* Poetics." Unpublished manuscript, April 24, 2017, Microsoft Word file.

———. "The Story of Sagoromo and Asukai." In *Traditional Japanese Literature, an Anthology: Beginnings to 1600*, ed. Haruo Shirane, 505–18. New York: Columbia University Press, 2006.

Dutcher, David. "*Sagoromo*, Co-Winner 2014 Kyoko Selden Memorial Translation Prize." *Japan Focus* 14, no. 19 (2016): 1–19.

Ebersole, Gary L. "The Poetics and Politics of Ritualized Weeping in Early and Medieval Japan." In *Holy Tears: Weeping in the Religious Imagination*, edited by Kimberley Christine Patton and John Stratton Hawley, 25–51. Princeton, NJ: Princeton University Press, 2018.

Faure, Bernard. *The Power of Denial: Buddhism, Purity, and Gender.* Princeton, NJ: Princeton University Press, 2003.

Goff, Janet Emily. *Noh Drama and "The Tale of the Genji": The Art of Allusion in Fifteen Classical Plays.* Princeton, NJ: Princeton University Press, 2014.

Hambrick, Charles H. "The *Gukanshō*: A Religious View of Japanese History." *Japanese Journal of Religious Studies* 5, no. 1 (March 1978): 37–58.

Hanna, Steven. "Hemmed in: Plotting and Constriction." Unpublished manuscript, April 24, 2017. Microsoft Word file.

———, trans. "The Tale of Sagoromo." Unpublished manuscript, April 20, 2021. Microsoft Word file.

Harper, Thomas, and Haruo Shirane, eds. *Reading "The Tale of Genji": Sources from the First Millennium*. New York: Columbia University Press, 2015.

Horton, H. Mack. "Portrait of a Medieval Japanese Marriage: The Domestic Life of Sanjōnishi Sanetaka and His Wife." *Japanese Language and Literature* 37, no. 2 (October 2003): 130–54.

Kamens, Edward. *Utamakura, Allusion, and Intertextuality in Traditional Japanese Poetry*. New Haven, CT: Yale University Press, 1997.

Klein, Susan Blakeley. *Allegories of Desire: Esoteric Literary Commentaries of Medieval Japan*. Cambridge, MA: Harvard University Asia Center, 2003.

Li, Michelle Osterfeld. *Ambiguous Bodies: Reading the Grotesque in Japanese Setsuwa Tales*. Stanford: Stanford University Press, 2009.

Lim, Beng Choo. *Another Stage: Kanze Nobumitsu and the Late Muromachi Noh Theater*. Ithaca, NY: Cornell East Asia Series, 2012.

Marra, Michele. "*Mumyōzōshi*, Part 2." *Monumenta Nipponica* 39, no. 3 (Autumn 1984): 281–305.

McCormick, Melissa. *Tosa Mitsunobu and the Small Scroll in Medieval Japan*. Seattle: University of Washington Press, 2009.

McCullough, Helen Craig. *Kokin Wakashū: The First Imperial Anthology of Japanese Poetry*. Stanford: Stanford University Press, 1985.

McCullough, H. William and Helen Craig McCullough, *A Tale of Flowering Fortunes: Annals of Japanese Aristocratic Life in the Heian Period*. 2 vols. Stanford: Stanford University Press, 1980.

Mostow, Joshua S., and Royall Tyler. *The Ise Stories: Ise monogatari*. Honolulu: University of Hawai'i Press, 2010.

Newhard, Jamie L. *Knowing the Amorous Man: A History of Scholarship on Tales of Ise*. Cambridge, MA: Harvard University Asia Center, 2013.

Owen, Stephen. *The Late Tang: Chinese Poetry of the Mid-Ninth Century (827–860)*. Cambridge, MA: Harvard University Asia Center, 2006.

Paludi, Michele A., and J. Harold Ellens, eds. *Feminism and Religion: How Faiths View Women and Their Rights*. Santa Barbara, CA: Praeger, 2016.

Pollack, David. *The Fracture of Meaning: Japan's Synthesis of China from the Eighth through the Eighteenth Centuries*. 1986. Reprint, Princeton, NJ: Princeton University Press, 2017.

Ramirez-Christensen, Esperanza. *Murmured Conversations: A Treatise on Poetry and Buddhism by the Poet-Monk Shinkei*. Stanford: Stanford University Press, 2008.

Reider, Noriko T. "A Demon in the Sky: The Tale of Amewakamiko, a Japanese Medieval Story." *Marvels & Tales* 29, no. 2 (July 2015): 265–82.

Rimer, J. Thomas, and Jonathan Chaves. *Japanese and Chinese Poems to Sing*. New York: Columbia University Press, 1997.

Rodd, Laurel Rasplica. *Kokinshū: A Collection of Poems Ancient and Modern*. Boston: Cheng & Tsui, 1996.

——. *Shinkokinshū: A New Collection of Poems Ancient and Modern*. 2 vols. Leiden: Brill, 2015.

Ruch, Barbara. "Medieval Jongleurs and the Making of a National Literature." In *Japan in the Muromachi Age*, edited by John Whitney Hall and Toyoda Takeshi, 279–309. 1977. Reprint, Ithaca, NY: Cornell East Asia Series, 2001.

Ruch, Barbara. "The Other Side of Culture in Medieval Japan." In *The Cambridge History of Japan*, edited by Kozo Yamamura, 500–43. Cambridge: Cambridge University Press, 1990.

Shirane, Haruo. "Lyricism and Intertextuality: An Approach to Shunzei's Poetics." *Harvard Journal of Asiatic Studies* 50, no. 1 (June 1990): 71–85.

Soka Gakkai Dictionary of Buddhism. Soka Gakkai Nichiren Buddhism Library. https://www.nichirenlibrary.org/en/dic/toc/.

Teeuwen, Mark. "The Kami in Esoteric Buddhist Thought and Practice." In *Shinto in History: Ways of the Kami*, edited by John Breen and Mark Teeuwen, 95–116. Honolulu: University of Hawai'i Press, 2000.

Tonomura, Hitomi. "Coercive Sex in the Medieval Japanese Court: Lady Nijō's Memoir." *Monumenta Nipponica* 61, no. 3 (Autumn 2006): 283–338.

Tyler, Royall, trans. *The Tale of Genji*. 2 vols. New York: Viking, 2001.

Ueki, Masatoshi. *Gender Equality in Buddhism*. New York: Peter Lang, 2001.

Uraki, Ziro, trans. *The Tale of the Cavern*. Tokyo: Shinozaki Shorin, 1984.

Vieillard-Baron, Michel. "New Worlds: Matching and Recontextualizing Poetry Excerpted from Fiction in the *Monogatari Niyakuban Utaawase*." *Cipango: French Journal of Japanese Studies* 3 (2014). http://cjs.revues.org/557.

Watson, Burton. *The Lotus Sutra*. New York: Columbia University Press, 1993.

INDEX

Abutsu, 20
aimite wa, 53
aki no iro wa, 61
aki no yo no, 106
ama no to o, 53, 77n35
Amaterasu, 2, 15–16, 46, 94n50
Amewakamiko, 9, 15–16, 17, 71n8, 71–72n9,
   119n101
Amida Buddha, 46n75
Anraku Temple, 37
Arashiyama, 90n36
Ariwara Narihira, 72n14
Ashikaga Yoshihisa, 21, 80
Ashikaga Yoshizumi, 22
Asukagawa, 76n33
Asukai
   brought back from dead, 44–45
   exhumation of, 43–44
   importance of relationship with, 10
   longing and, 19
   as nun, 46
   plotline involving, 11–12, 14–15, 21n57
   in *The Sagoromo Middle Captain* (*Sagoromo
      no chūjō*), 29–35, 37–39, 41, 43–46
   in *Sagoromo: The Wisconsin Collection*,
      52–56, 59–61, 63, 67
   in *"Sagoromo's Skirts"* (*Sagoromo no tsuma*),
      75–79
   in *Sagoromo's Undersash* (*Sagoromo no shita-
      himo*), 116n89
Asukai no, 29
"Autumn View of Chang'an" (Zhao Gu),
   91n38
aware sou, 66
Awataguchi, 28

Bai Juyi, 8, 91n40
Baishi, Princess, 7
Bangai yōkyoku gojūichiban, 80
Bishamon, 47
boats, 17–18
Brahma's Net Sutra, 108

chigiri araba, 36
Chūko kayō enkyoku zenshū (Yoshida), 68
Cloak of Invisibility, The (*Kakuremino*), 110n60
Cloistered Princess (*Nyūdō no Miya*), 13–14
clothing
   banquet songs and, 19, 22
   emphasis on, 15
   robes, 9–10, 15, 19, 22
   Undersash and, 24
   wisteria robes (*fujigoromo*), 30–31n21, 31
Collection of Ancient and Modern Japanese
   Poems (*Kokin wakashū* or *Kokinshū*), 16,
   18, 27n2, 86n16, 87n22, 102n30, 108n53
Collection of Gleanings of Japanese Poems (*Shūi
   wakashū*), 72n11, 93n48, 100, 111n61
Collection of Ten Thousand Leaves
   (*Man'yōshū*), 101n29, 110n60
Collection of Verbal Flowers (*Shikashū*), 111n61
Collection of Wind-Blown Leaves (*Fūyō
   wakashū*), 18, 23, 48–49
common culture, 4n11
Continued Collection of Ancient and Modern
   Japanese Poems (*Shoku Kokin wakashū*),
   82n6, 101n29, 107n52

Daibutsu, 39n55
Daini no Sanmi, 97n13
Dainichi, 46

earthquakes, 16
en, 8
Enkyoku jūshichi chō (Yoshida), 68
Enkyokushō (Treatise on Banquet Songs), 20, 68
enlightenment, women and, 85n14
Enyū, Emperor, 97

failed relationships, 3
Flower Garland Sutra, 108
Fudō, 46
Fugen, 12
fujigoromo kitaru mi nareba kakure nashi, 30
fujigoromo kitaru mi nareba osore nashi, 31

CPSIA information can be obtained
at www.ICGtesting.com
Printed in the USA
LVHW101824230922
729126LV00002B/72